Margot — *[inscription]*
on your journey!

Tom *[signature]*
2019

War Stories 2017

"Life is pain, highness. Anyone who says differently is selling something."

— William Goldman, *The Princess Bride*

"Life is pain, princess."

— Sean Davis, Post 134

Contents

I Was High

by Jacob Meeks

Chandler, Arizona – Fall 1999

Davy and I strolled down the street with a massive cloud of invisible pot smoke seemingly enveloping us in a haze. We're both stoned and on another planet. Davy's on his. He's happy, laughing and joking. I'm on mine. I'm quiet. Paranoid. Brooding. I don't like being high. I have social anxiety. Pot makes it worse. I only smoke it because people told me it would make me cool. I don't think I buy that.

We walk into this plaza. It's just a bunch of stores and shops. My brain is going this way and that.

What am I doing with my life? I left my home in Wyoming a year and a half ago, right after I turned eighteen, without even telling my parents. I was pissed at them. Teenage angst. I barely graduated high school because I had to cram a bunch of credits into a few months to make it in a new state. I've been bouncing around ever since. Wyoming to New Mexico back to Wyoming and now in Arizona for the last year.

It's been nothing but booze and drugs. Mostly I smoke pot and drink. I've tried other things, though. I smoked crack with a Sammy Hagar impersonator. Him and his cracked-out buddies got all paranoid on me. Did a bunch of coke. Tried to score meth from a Mexican gangster who was also a Golden Gloves boxer, talked shit to him and got half my face torn off. Did some ecstasy, a pure form of it, did so much it slowed my heart rate down to a point where I passed out and Davy thought it stopped my heart. Did acid, tripped out and hung out by the pool with a bunch of crazy spider monkeys. All kinds of stuff. I don't know what I'm doing with my life.

I'm working at Wal-Mart. I unload trucks and stock the shelves during the graveyard shift. I used to work in pets. That sucked. Except when I would get high and pass out behind a wall of dog food bags. Then they moved me to electronics. It's better. At least you get customers now and then. They gave me Employee of the Month a few months back. Got a twenty-five-dollar gift certificate. Bought me a Metallica CD.

It's still better than it used to be. Not that long ago, I was selling plasma twice a week so I could pay for food and cigarettes. I was shoplifting petty stuff all the time. Lucky I never got caught. It's all because I'm an idiot that chose to leave home with no plan, no nothing. I'm good at school but I didn't have any friends, no social skills to speak of, wasn't very popular. Everything in small town America when you're young is about being popular. I wasn't.

I start looking around the plaza. Thinking, *Damn, I really need to do something with my life. I have to be somebody. I can't go on like this forever. What am I going to do? Who am I going to be?* I'm having a crisis in the soul.

Finally, my eyes pause. I see a Marine recruiting office on one side of the plaza. I shake my head. I think to myself, *Man, I can't swim for shit.*

Then I see an Army recruiter on the other side of the plaza. That's it! That's my ticket out.

When I was a child, I always thought the Army was for stupid people. Hell, my whole family joined the military and they all hated it. I said I was never going to go.

I have to go, though. I have to be somebody. I have to become a man.

"Davy! Hold up. I'm going to go inside and talk to the Army recruiter."

Davy retorts, "What the fuck are you talking about?"

"You heard me, I want to go talk to the recruiter." I leave Davy before he can say another word and head on inside.

I sit in the chair. I don't know how much time passes.

Finally, a man comes to me, his name was Staff Sergeant Hicks. He looks like a nice guy, he's like a poor man's Nicholas Cage. My eyes are blood shot as I sit down and tell him I want to join the Army. He goes straight into his spiel. I can't hear any of it. Too far gone. Then he shows me a video, a bunch of badass looking soldiers on rafts infiltrating a position, doing badass shit.

I think, *Yeah, I want to be like those guys. Where do I sign up?*

Sergeant Hicks stares at me intently the entire time. Finally, he asks, "Son, do you do drugs?"

I shift back in my seat a little bit and think to myself, *I don't really see the point in lying.*

I reply, "Honestly, I'm high right now."

Sergeant Hicks smiles and slaps his hand on his leg, "Don't worry about that!" he exclaims. "We've got a job for you!"

In my mind, I'm not too worried. I know this is the path. For the longest time I've been wandering around, thinking about how I could possibly become a man. After watching those guys in the rafts, I found my way.

Or maybe it was just the pot talking.

***

Postscript ~ Almost a year later

It took me some time to get clean and join. I finished basic training and airborne school. I had become an Airborne Infantryman. Sergeant Hicks, my recruiter, had asked me if I was sure when I said that I wanted to be infantry. He said I scored high enough on the ASVAB[1] to do whatever I wanted in the Army.

I was adamant. I wanted to be a man. I wanted to be like those guys in the rafts. I wanted to be Infantry. I ended up in Fort Bragg, home of the 82nd Airborne Division and the second largest US Army base in the country.

In my first week at the unit, I experienced my first mandatory fun day. The Army likes to use oxymorons like mandatory fun. How can something be mandatory, yet fun at the same time? It doesn't make sense.

On this day, each platoon of around eleven men was tasked with rowing twenty-three miles down Cape Fear in North Carolina. It was a hot August day. My platoon got the crappiest, oldest raft of the lot. I swear they had duct taped that thing together.

There was no current on the water. We started at 6:00 a.m. and all we did was row and row and row and row. It seemed never ending. The only things that broke the monotony of the day were watching a

---

[1] Armed Services Vocational Aptitude Battery

crocodile push himself into the water and a man with a huge confederate flag hanging from his trailer yelling something about the Latino man that was in our group. Not sure what he was yelling, but I don't think it was friendly.

Finally, two miles away from the end, it started raining, just pissing rain. We all became drenched. It looked like at one point we might have to capsize the raft and swim for it.

As the rain came down and covered us in water and just plain sucking, one of my new Sergeants looked over at me and shook his head with pity, realizing that I had just gotten to the unit.

He said, "Meeks, poor Meeks. This sucks for you. But yeah, I hate to tell you. It doesn't get any better than this."

He was right. It didn't get much better.

It was still a good move overall, but I can say, maybe I should have laid off the drugs, not taken the raft video to heart, and thought a little more about what it actually meant to be a man.

Welcome to Combat

by Damon Hugh Faust

There is a moment when all senses become in tune, when time stops and the sounds become amplified, every droplet of sweat is felt, the weight of your vest becomes non-existent as you become one with your gear: rifle an extension of your arm, the Humvee an extension of legs, your fire team are cells and organs of the same body. Not only have you become one with your body and the world around you, but you and your fire team are one.

WELCOME TO COMBAT SON. YOU WILL NEVER BE THE SAME!

In this moment, you no longer jump out of your skin at celebratory fire, fatigue is a distant memory along with sleep.

In these moments, a blast that brings debris rippling your way, filling the air with dust, obscuring your vision and sucking, craving, grasping for all the oxygen the blast devours; the same oxygen your lungs fight for. You are still present, you are carnage, you are destruction. And if by happenstance you drive through such a moment and find yourself intact, find yourself whole, you react.

Return fire. Suppress any potential targets. Call in location. Get QRF moving your direction.

Check self for wounds.
Check team for wounds.
Check status of trucks in convoy.
Charlie Mike, continue mission.

THE DESPERATE TIMES

by Josh Lubin

A speeding car slams into a telephone pole
on Powell Boulevard.
  Krista just OD'd.
I live across the street
  from a trap house.
A young girl stands on the front lawn screaming,
"Whose dick do I have to suck to get twenty bucks?"

The Republicans debate tonight. *I don't foresee any survivors.*

A long, hot line of traffic rubbernecks an accident.
  Tami OD'd last spring.
She was obsessed with Jeff Buckley, and
like a captain on a doomed ship, she considered
drowning   *a romantic and an honorable way to die.*

> Last night
> my friend's wife
> cornered me in my bar,
> pleading for advice
> on how to quit drinking.

> There's a new
> bridge in Portland,
> and the countdown has begun
> on who will be its first jumper.

> Today at my bar, a vase
> full of dahlias are starting to wither.
> *I am desperately trying to incorporate more*
> *images of flowers in my poetry.*

2

Recently I fell in love,
but I had a dream last night –

that we were all birds in flight,
hovering above the unkempt lawns
of America, waiting for a dick or drink
to swallow, for when the crash finally comes.

3

And I've seen
the HIV clinics in strip malls,
out, behind the beauty supply stores,
    in LA, out on
    MLK Jr. Boulevard,
    where Larz got his positive results,
    stole some mascara, decided to keep blooming,
    then hopped a bus back to the bathhouse.
On Craigslist he says,
the little bud for sale between his legs
is bigger and brighter than any Georgia O'Keeffe painting.

No mirrors / No smoke / Here, hope

Is lost / Is found

In a glory hole / In a bathroom stall

And I too leapt into it,
into it all; into a mad rush
of pavement and knockabout,
into the interior, away from New York,

into an uneasy America –

**and I came out on the other side
with battle scars and lousy jokes.**

4

And I saw the wannabe starlets
heading West on Greyhound buses,
and each one nearly broke me with their
beauty, checking their cherry red lipstick
in the back seat of the bus, next to screaming
                           children and working men,
   waiting to be discovered, like Marilyn Monroe,
                              like Dorothy Stratton,
like Haley's Comet, kissing celluloid so close, the film
                        just melted and split across the sky

And I've spoken
of the paper swans,

and there's no solace
in any cigarettes or sex.

These streets are a mess of
rush-hour humps. *And sport-fuck is the new 40.*

5

We are both built of the same damages; you and I.

Left-swipe / Right-swipe
Tinder / Grinder / FetLife

a) Binge drink and wink

to ease the bargaining and loss.

b) Hotel room tryst
  requires an electronic key calling card.

c) Pin it to your chest, to
  your bruises, like a purple heart.

This is where absentee fathers posing
as grave robbers have left no map where

      X marks *this spot* –

so, blink once for yes, and twice
  for no.   *Left-swipe / Right-swipe*
It's exactly how a burn victim communicates
on life support.
So we don't talk
about talking here – not when
we can let *our voices,*
        our bodies
be stripped down like prostitutes
  who learned the hard way how   *not to scream.*

6

Sabotage, like
gravity, is and always
will be such a powerful thing.

But we are so subtle, so casual *about this* –
subtle as a white suburban kid with dreadlocks
who just discovered hip hop.
Subtle as a train wreck.

Subtle as the limp Sieg Heil of a casual racist.

Pray for a want.
Pray for a wish.
Pray for a tissue
to wipe away the evidence;
the stranger's cum, the tainted blood,
the tell-tale tracks inside an arm crutch
you didn't mean to expose to the cashier-clerk
in the supermarket.

Pray for a pink cloud, a pink hole, and a Percocet.
Pray for an Ok Cupid foxhole to fall into and finally find God.

Fall from grace or fall in love – *here* –
we are the suicides, the most attractive ones,
collecting lucky stars all the way down.

Here, hope

Is a thief's prayer / Is a Facebook apology / Is innocent till you
get caught

Is living in tilt under the care of self-providence till the day is
done

7

And the world can go on,
with its dying pop stars, aging
rock stars, popular writers   *and republicans.*

With its rent hikes and regular blues.
With its nouveau riche and no-class citizens.
With its alt-lit art boys, mad dogs   *and boxed wine.*

With its shirtless shopping cart citizens;
denizens of daybreak, taking pass-out naps
                    in the afternoon alley shade.

With its bus stop starlets, 16 and pregnant,
a generation of Botox stillborns, all fading fast
in bleach-blonde dye-jobs   *and cheap push-up bras.*

With its discount rack cougars, slumming the aisles
of TJ Max,
Chico's and Ross.

With its bargaining and loss.

With its fucking
and fighting, its Doms and Subs,
and consensual restraining orders.

With its bruises shaped like purple hearts.

With its genders fluid as flash floods,
tossing pronouns around, up into the air
like glitter, like wartime confetti over the
            befuddled, closet-building masses.

And the world can go on –

with its *love and love and love,*
and needing,
and sad pandas,
and sinking Ophelia's
who never learned how to *breathe.*
There are no limits to modern love. *No survivors.*

Take this key,
this heart, this body,
this canvas; *take me, use me.*

"I want you to own me." She said.

8

Even Sylvia Plath had daddy issues,
and these are still the desperate times.

9

A speeding car slams
into a telephone pole on Powell Boulevard.

Krista just OD'd.
Tami OD'd last spring.

Larz derails from his tracks,
hovering like a Venus Flytrap inside

a perfumed clam shell, as Jeff Buckley's
body floats down the Mississippi, out into the sea.

> Recently I fell in love,
> and I had a dream last night –
> that we all were birds in flight,
> hovering above the unkempt lawns
> of America, barely keeping our heads
> above water, where we abandoned nothing –

but hope   is bought / is sold / is bargained / is lost

inside a four-chambered room
that beats above the pumping blood
and memory   of walls.

These are still the desperate times.

Abandon nothing   but your ghosts.

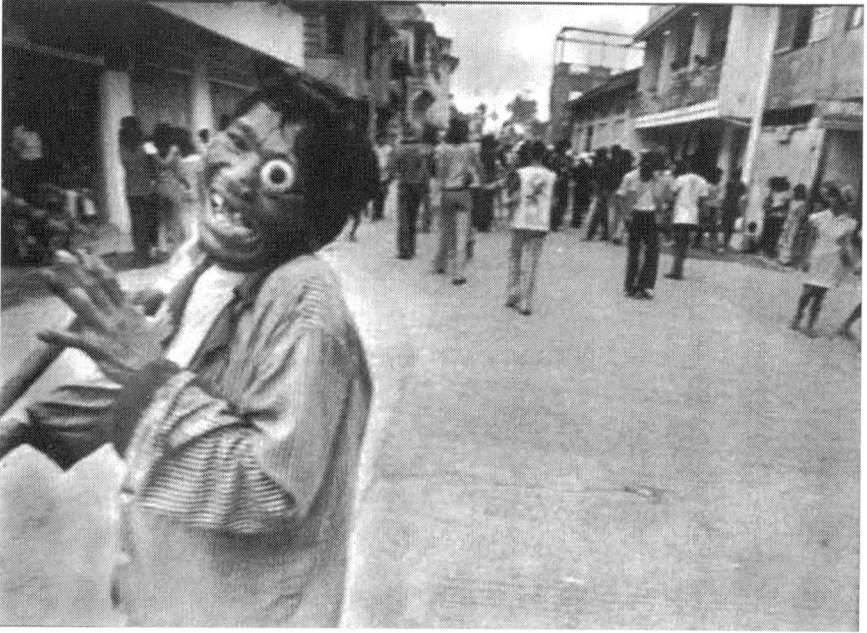

Photo by Joe Cantrell

War Secrets

by Jana Mowreader

A child's memory

I am in first grade. Every week we practice duck and cover. At first, I pretended I was looking for ducks. Then I understood that this was not a game. I heard my teacher Mrs. Baker talking to someone about the bombs that ended the war and turned cities to ash. I wasn't supposed to laugh during duck and cover.

Asking questions gets me in trouble. Especially if Mama is wearing her mean face. I don't want to be in trouble. I guess she doesn't like me very much. She doesn't give me hugs or kind words like some mothers do. I don't talk much or make noise. I spend a lot to time watching – or hiding.

One day, Mama tells me my Papa will be coming home from the war. Mama tells me I'd better be a good girl and not bother him.

I lurk in corners, in the hallway, behind the couch. Listening to whispered conversations.

Mama on the phone.

Cities vanishing.

Ash.

I'm afraid of radios. Quietly, I unplug them so they cannot be radioactive. Why am I the only one to do this?

My father is tall. I call him Papa. Papa is different. He doesn't have a mean face like Mama – just a sad face. An empty face. On the best days, he laughs and swings me up in the air. Sometimes he lets me help him in his workshop in the basement. He's good at fixing things. Some days, he is silent. Just staring. I have learned it is not good to surprise him.

Mama nags all the time. *Why doesn't he do this. Why doesn't he do that.*

Papa went to work, then he got a second job in the evenings. He's gone a lot. I get up in the morning and set the table for him. If the milk bottle is not full, I can carry it to the table. I help him make his sandwiches. If I have candy I put some in his lunch bag. It is just him and me in the morning. He likes cream in his coffee and he lets me have a sip. When he leaves, I put his dishes in the sink and rinse them. At night, I have to go to bed before he gets home. When he does get home, I hear Mama complaining. I hear them fighting.

Will he go away again?

I would.

Now I practice duck and cover quietly at home, in my room, in the basement, in the yard beneath the shrubs. In the back seat of the car. I'm good at duck and cover, but how will I know when it is time for it if I'm not near Mrs. Baker?

Was Papa there? Is this what Mama whispered about to her friends? Ash and disappeared cities. Is this why Papa doesn't talk or smile much?

Uncle Emmett and Aunt Hattie come to dinner most Sundays. Aunt Hattie always brings dessert. Sometimes pies, sometimes bread pudding with caramel sauce.

Uncle's face and neck and arm are melted on one side. He has a pirate patch over his eye. Some of his fingers are gone. The ones left are skinny and crooked and don't bend.

I'm not supposed to stare.

His good side smiles. I sit on his good side and pat his arm.

Mama always wants me to wear a bandage on my hand with the bad scar where I got burned with hot jelly. Even though it's healed and doesn't hurt any more. Mama was making jelly and I wanted to help stir. Mama wanted me to leave her alone. She got mad, pulled the spoon out of the kettle and slammed it down. A blob of hot jelly flew up and fell on my hand. One Sunday I decided not to wear the bandage at dinner. Why should I hide such a little scar when Uncle had such big scars?

Uncle reached over and gently touched my scar.

After that, I made sure to sit on the melted side. I like holding his melted hand when grace is said. I like how hard the skin feels where it's ridged with white and red. I'm careful not to touch too hard.

After dinner, I sometimes go for a walk with Uncle Emmett. He walks slow. He breathes funny. His voice is raspy.

I tell him how I got my scar from hot jelly. Then I ask him how he got his.

He says he was on a ship in the Navy and it got torpedoed. His says a torpedo is a kind of bomb. An explosion threw him up into the air and then into the water. The water was on fire.

I don't understand how water could be on fire.

I remember how much my little burn had hurt and I think about how much bigger his burns are and how much more he must have hurt. I start to cry and hug his leg. He says I am his little sunshine friend. I love him.

Later, I take some matches from the kitchen drawer and try to light a bowl of water on fire but it doesn't work. The match always goes out.

Sometimes after dinner Uncle and Papa go out to the garage where Papa keeps a bottle of light brown juice on a high shelf behind a bucket of nuts and bolts. He doesn't know I know, but I'm good at watching. It tastes nasty. When I have my own house, I will find out where to buy it and I'll keep it in the kitchen so they don't have to go out to the garage to drink it.

Out in the garage is where Uncle Emmett and Papa talk about the war. Uncle Emmett was in the Navy. Once he talked about the oil spreading over the water and burning. He talked about swimming under the water and trying to get away from the fire. When he couldn't hold his breath any more he would reach up and try to sweep away the flames to make a place to breathe. He talks about how hot the air was. He talks about Pearl. Papa talks about the Army and the Pacific theatre.

I didn't know that wars had theaters.

A sister's memory

My best friend ever is my baby brother Davy. I remember when we went to the hospital to bring him home. He was the most amazing thing I had ever seen. I get to hold him a lot because he stops crying when I hold him and rock him. I learn how to give him his bottle and burp him.

I almost never bring anybody home with me. I don't know how my mother will be – angry and sad, or full of energy and silly. I like the angry and sad better because when she's full of energy it can change to angry at any minute with no warning. When she's sad sometimes she'll sleep most of the day – then I can read and play with Davy.

I am afraid of her.

I don't want people to see that she doesn't act like other mothers. It is more important to be with Davy – to make sure he is safe. I make sure he doesn't do anything to get spanked. Or slapped.

We play in the ravine and at the river. We collect frogs and salamanders and sometimes little mice. We have lots of adventures building forts and digging caves. We both like to read and tell each other stories. I'm not as afraid of Ma now. She can hit me all she wants, as long as she doesn't hit Davy.

I guess I am a really bad person like she says. I hope Papa and Davy don't find out. I'm afraid they might stop loving me.

A young woman's memory

In college, we hear a lot about Vietnam. Boys I knew from school get drafted and go to boot camp, then to war. I know more, read more, understand more about war. Things I remember from my childhood make more sense.

I understand that my two cousins who didn't come back from Korea died.

I understood that Uncle Emmett had been hurt bad in my Papa's war. My cousin, Loren, had started to drink a lot and get into fights when he got home from Korea. After a while he stopped coming home. I hear he's living on the streets.

Davy has graduated from high school and sometimes talks about the draft. One weekend, Davy tells me he has a secret he isn't ready to share with Papa and Ma yet. He tells me he didn't want to be drafted into the Army, so he signed up with the Marines. If he's going to war, he wants to be the baddest badass he can be. He leaves for boot camp in two weeks.

I think about how unhappy Papa was. I think about Uncle Emmett and his burns – how he died a few years ago in pain, coughing. I think about my cousins that didn't come back from Korea. I think about Loren and how he changed. About Loren's brother Edward who seems mostly okay. One out of six that I know and love seems to have a good life.

Mostly, I think about Davy and how I would live if he goes to war and doesn't come back. I've never had a friend I cared for as much as him. We tell each other our secrets and dreams. Being his friend is the only thing I'm good at. I don't think I would want to live if he wasn't in my world.

We know now that Ma has a mental illness that leads to unhappiness and that is why she blames everyone for making her miserable. She's never said she was sorry for being so mean. I read there was medication that would help, but she doesn't want to hear about it. Once, Davy said she needed a psychiatrist. That was one of the few times she hit him. It was all somehow my fault, Papa's fault, and sometimes Davy's.

I love Papa and Davy. I know Papa drinks more often but I think I would drink, too, if I had to deal with Ma. Drinking never made him angry – in fact, he's more relaxed when he's had a drink. He never seems drunk but has a drink every couple of hours.

I always escaped by studying, reading, babysitting and later working. I helped make sure Davy had someplace to be when I wasn't home. I could never bear the idea that he would be hurt by Ma or anyone else.

I spent days trying to figure out what I would do if he goes to war and doesn't come back. I don't think I could live with that.

I tape a long stick to the back of my leg and spend a day walking with a crutch to see what it might be like to walk with a knee that wouldn't bend. Next, I put a piece of broken coke bottle in my shoe and spend a day walking without being able to put any weight on that foot. Then, I go to the library and find where all the big arteries are in the legs. I think he might not be my friend anymore, but he would be alive. I could live with that.

I know where Papa's handgun is. I'm good at watching. I know where the bullets are. I think I could keep one person I love from being destroyed by war.

How Bright It Is[2]

By Brian Turner

April. And the air dry
as the shoulders of a water buffalo.

Grasshoppers scratch at the dirt,
rub their wings with thin legs,
flaring out in front of the soldiers
in low arcing flights, wings a blur.

The soldiers don't notice anymore,
seeing only the wreckage of the streets,
bodies draped with sheets, and the sun,
how bright it is, how hard and flat and white.

It will take many nails from the coffinmakers
to shut out this light, which reflects off everything:
the calloused feet of the dead, their bony hands,
their pale foreheads so cold, brilliant in the sun.

---

[2] From *Here, Bullet* - Alice James Books 2005

A Convoy for the *Con Voi*

by Tom Keating

In 1969, I was re-assigned to a headquarters unit of a large logistics support base, at Long Binh Post, northeast of Saigon.

Enemy artillery shelled us regularly, and they were constantly trying to attack us with commando raids. One got used to the alert sirens, crouching in sand-bagged bunkers, waiting for the mortar or 122-millimeter rocket attacks to end, hearing the all-clear sirens, then climbing out of the bunker to return to work, which in my case, was typing construction contracts for US firms to build more military bases in-country. I was one of the many "support troops." Rear Echelon Mother Fuckers, the grunts called us. We lived on large bases, relatively safe and in comfort. Hot food, plenty of water, only pulling bunker guard duty or small sweeps outside the wire.

I wasn't on the job long when my commanding officer called in and said, "Keating, go with Joe and get my elephants."

"Sir?" I asked, puzzled. He looked at me for a second, then he remembered I was the new guy. He explained.

The Colonel was leaving Vietnam soon and had ordered some decorative, ceramic elephants from a local factory to bring home to Georgia. These elephants were made of china or clay, fired and glazed and brightly colored. They were hollow like a chocolate Easter bunny. They stood about one meter high and people used them as plant stands in their homes. GIs called them BUFEs, Big Ugly Fucking Elephants, and my colonel wanted me to drive to the factory somewhere in the countryside, pick up the elephants and bring them back to his quarters before he went home.

The local factory was about fifteen clicks from our base. It was in the middle of nowhere, and near an US Army combat base. Shit, that was not good. I knew that combat bases were always located where the enemy was most active in an area.

Joe, an E-5 SGT who had been there on other trips, was going to be the driver. The idea was to show me the way to the factory so I could do the next trip for the officers. While he signed out the jeep, I put four canteens of water in the back and signed out our weapons. We joined a small MP truck convoy that was going to the combat base near the factory.

The convoy commander, a young lieutenant[3] called all the drivers together to go over the basic rules of the convoy. "Keep your interval between vehicles. Don't let any fucking gook vehicles in the convoy, or ARVNs[4], either. Never stop, no matter what. If fired on, speed up and get the fuck out of the kill zone. Got it?"

Everyone nodded. Convoys were always targets. The truck drivers and their relief drivers carried M-16 automatic rifles. They sat on their armor-plated flak jackets as extra protection against what are nowadays call IEDs, but back then we called them command detonated mines. They strapped on their steel pots. Joe and I did the same.

Our convoy went out the main gate of the base, the LT in the lead in his jeep with its M-60 machine gun on the mount. Another jeep brought up the rear, also with a machine gunner.

I thought, *nobody back home would believe that I was in an armed convoy going to an enemy-held area to get fucking ceramic elephants for an officer's mid-century ranch-style house in Georgia. Great.*

---

[3] L.T.
[4] Army of Republic of Vietnam

As we turned onto Highway 1, Joe pointed out an elderly, bearded Vietnamese man wearing a NON-LA, the famous Asian conical hat made of reeds, sitting by the side of the road.

"See that Papa-san?" he said. "He's counting the vehicles in this convoy. He'll report to the VC how many vehicles we have, and where we're heading, north or south. There's a gook at every exit on the post."

I looked over at the old man - he was using his Buddhist beads to count our trucks.

The convoy moved slowly. The tropical sun beat on us, but the slight breeze as we drove gave us some relief. We had travelled about one kilometer into the trip, when I heard a sharp screeching sound up ahead, then a blaring truck horn, followed by a loud crunch. The convoy sped up. We did the same.

As we zipped ahead, I saw a crushed Vespa motor scooter in the middle of the road.

One of the trucks in the convoy had run over it. It must have slipped between the trucks. I didn't see the Vespa driver, but there was a lot of blood on the road, and a smear of blood led off to the shoulder where a cluster of Vietnamese was shouting at the convoy.

"Dung Lai! Dung Lai!"[5]

Nobody stopped.

We drove on.

---

[5] "Stop! Stop!"

An hour later, Joe turned off the highway and onto a rut-filled dirt road, red dust spilling behind us. We were in the boonies, someplace in the middle of rice paddies and jungle. The elephant "factory" was a low rambling one-story structure made from sheets of corrugated metal. Two ceramic elephants were standing on either side of the entrance. A hand-painted sign in Vietnamese said CON VOI[6] over the entrance.

Joe parked the jeep and entered the factory to check on our elephants while I stood guard at the jeep in the hot sun. I took off my helmet, and put on my boonie hat and was drinking from a canteen when some Vietnamese kids from the little village next to the factory gathered around the jeep. They were all thin, black haired and smiling. They asked for cigarettes with the universal sign language of two fingers at the mouth. I obliged and passed out my Marlboros.

One kid, he looked about seven years old, begged for a cigarette and I gave him one. I laughed when he whipped out a Zippo lighter to light his buddies' cigarettes.

I showed them a magic trick I learned from watching old Laurel and Hardy movies, where Stan would seem to take off his finger and put it back on. They shrieked and laughed at the trick and wanted me to do it again. They spoke no English, but, using my bad Vietnamese, I did get them to count, "*một, hai, ba*" before I put my finger back together a few more times.

Joe returned with the workers and they carefully placed our two brightly colored elephants into the jeep. After covering them with a canvas tarp, I gave the kids the rest of my Marlboros and we drove away.

---

[6] Elephant

It was getting late, and we didn't want to drive back to Long Binh Post alone, at night. Nighttime belonged to the VC. We checked in at the combat base near the factory for the night. The MP at the gate told us to keep our weapons handy. Intel indicated possible enemy activity.

We didn't get much sleep that night, awakened by artillery fire and the sound of flares popping into the darkness, and the BRRAPPP! of mini guns firing red lines of bullets down from gunships onto some poor bastards outside the perimeter.

I guess Intel was right for once.

Our elephants were snug and covered in the back of the jeep.

When we left the base the next morning, sure enough, I saw an old man sitting outside the gate, watching and counting.

We returned to Long Binh Post and Joe drove to the officers' quarters where we dropped the elephants off at the Colonel's air-conditioned trailer. A few days later, he shipped his elephants home with him and left Vietnam. But before he left, the colonel wrote recommendations for medals for both of us for getting the elephants.

His words were "For Hazardous duty" on the citation. Thankfully, higher headquarters denied the recommendations. It would be so embarrassing to have to tell people, "And I got this medal here for delivering plant stands."

I never had to drive back to the factory, the village, and the kids. The factory owner started selling his elephants in a shop on our base not long after that first trip. He was doing great business when I went home three months later - without any elephants.

Photo by Joe Cantrell

Words We Need In English

hiraeth

Language: **Welsh**

A homesickness for a home to which you cannot return, a home which maybe never was; the nostalgia, the yearning, the grief for the lost places of your past. An earnest desire for the past.

toska

Language: **Russian**

Pure, unadulterated, heart-wrenching sadness.

"The sensation of great spiritual anguish, often without any specific cause. At less morbid levels it is a dull ache of the soul, a longing with nothing to long for, a sick pining, a vague restlessness, mental throes, yearning." – Vladimir Nabokov

dépaysement

Language: **French**

The feeling that comes from not being in one's home country.

litost

Language: **Czech**

A feeling that synthesizes grief, sympathy, remorse and longing.

ubuntu

Region: **Southern Africa**

The belief that we are defined by our compassion and kindness toward others.

heimat

Language: **German**

Refers to the place that makes us who we are, the attitudes and beliefs we've formed that have evolved over generations. It doesn't refer to just homeland pride, but roots. The place we're connected to that shaped who we are.

ذ ق برذي (To'oborni)

Language: **Arabic**

Word used for that person who you love so much that you would rather die than be on this earth without them.

"You bury me; I love you so much that I want to die before you."

And It Starts With A Scream

by Jonathan Oak

And it starts with a scream –
sound from a piston gone wild.
I didn't know a heart could open up so violently.
Membrane and muscle. Trembling 440 cycles.

I'm a big dumb animal,
and nothing I've ever seen or done with this life
would indicate otherwise.

It started down deep,
a yell rising from the pit of my stomach
and coated in viscous yellow,
echoing over 260 square feet of lung
and driving open the flood gates with sound.

I've been flooded with the lies and misconceptions
      of all the other big dumb animals.

And there's Brando in his cave
          waiting for the apocalypse to come.

The neck half opened, slanted forward,
I can see the separation of the meat as he stumbles.
     It's fresh
          and it's red
              and it's newly exposed
                    to the air and the oxygen.

Even the insides of big dumb animals like us
ain't supposed to be shorn from the bone
while we're still alive.

But this is the nature of revelation.
You don't get to ease into it gentle,
dipping your toes into the blood to see
                                    how cold it is.

It's the ice that's flung itself headlong
through the veins of heroes and killers
the distinction depending
on which side of which flag you're standing.

But distinctions be damned.
There's nothing to sacrifice but illusion.

There's fear so deep
          it can't be defined.
There's resolution so pure
          that choice is gone.
There's a hard drive
          spinning up the back of the brain

and the needle's gone haywire,
writing random bits, electromagnetic,
into the surface.
Crypto
          photo
                    holographic info

embedded with decrypt keys,
emblazoned upon raw neurons.

And there's a chance,
                    a small one,

I could rise above
      the empty,
          hacking,
             coughing,
                dying existence
of "big dumb animal."

And where it starts with a scream,
it finally ends once the steam has run out
and the engine seized in rust,
when my eyes have shut
to better see the inner turmoil,
my voice gone to rasping whispers
with the telling of thread-worn memory,
when the pain in my skull
has flashed up like powder,
the circuits fried out
and muscles gone slack,

when the time has come inevitably to this...

when 6 quarts of antifreeze
      have taken up residence in my veins
forcing 6 quarts of blood
      to fill the once hollowed cavity of my lungs,
forcing 6 quarts of air
      to spill out past my lips
                in frothing red flecks.

And I'm trembling, trembling,
rising up off that A above Middle C,
440 Hz screaming,
the notes of a new song
vomited out
in oxygen-rich red.

And the screaming becomes music again.
Everything is first times again!

Amazing!

Then
      finally
            it ends.

The Spinster's Tale

by Sigrid Casey
"The past is never dead. It's not even past." ~ William Faulkner

"Hey, thanks for calling," he said. "Gotta say bye now, time to feed the dog." Al said it like a fact, but wasn't talking about his boyhood pal, or the shepherd he had when he was married. They were all long gone.

"I wish you wouldn't talk about Mom that way," I said.

I didn't get into it with him, might as well talk to granite. And he didn't bother to justify, I knew his reasons. Besides, she'd given him all the cards years before: durable power of attorney, medical proxy, executor. Only thing I could do was report him, call in elder abuse. And that's what it was, mental. Asking every morning if she was planning on dying that day.

He resented her breathing. Couldn't stand listening to the same six stories over and over. Wouldn't watch her eat. Bathing her unendurable.

Most of this is bad memory and the rest speculative imagination. The few real facts are just too perfect to leave out, and it all locks up tighter than a jigsaw puzzle. How many generations inherit a family tattoo before it fades? You don't have to like the picture.

Mother was barely into infancy when her father, Albrecht, died in 1914. She always seemed proud that she and The Great War were born the same day. But since that's not an actual fact, maybe it went this way. When the War broke out, her father was already at the front, and when she was born, it was the same day he was shot. He died six weeks later, never saw her, never held her. Her life had been exchanged for his.

The real story goes like this: ever after in deep mourning, Grandma longed only for her own death to bring her soul to Heaven, where she'd be with her Albrecht again. The child was of some concern, but no particular solace. Grandma would have killed herself, except the sin would destroy her only hope. She told her daughter so when my Mother was seven or eight.

It was just a fact.

She was the only Grandma I knew, and when she died, the Devil visited my dreams with an offer. I could die instead of Grandma. Everyone would be so much happier. How could I, a worthless child, be so selfish not to agree?

Grandfather's death graved a mark upon Mother so profound it would have been less deep only had he lived. She bore painfully the burden of any deprivation her mother faced, especially those she herself had innocently caused. The lost piece of toast still grieved her. Mother was desperate to equal her father any way she could, and replace him any way she couldn't. As a child, one time she threw out her shoulder trying to match the power of his arm.

My brother was born when Mother was forty. Named for her father, Al hardly stood a chance.

When Al joined up at seventeen, I was living on the opposite coast. No telling what he'd done, but he'd been given the option of going to juvie or the army. With her namesake father-son in the army, Mother was in heaven herself. For this they'd played armies and soldiers when he was little. For this she'd waited all her life.

Our Dad, the pacifist, was less hearty: "If you have to, make sure the other guy dies."

And Al jumped into the 82nd Airborne.

He loved the army because it made sense. Why he didn't re-enlist I never knew. Afterwards, Al stayed pretty close to home. Sometimes living with Mother and Dad, inconsistently elsewhere, always dropping by with the laundry. Never officially living with a girlfriend. Mother doted on him. I've got a photo of the two of them when he was twenty-something. He's sitting up high on a sawn-off stump and smirking, she's in her fluffy pink robe, looking up and adoring. When he finally married at thirty-four, she wailed, "He's not mine anymore!"

The daughter-in-law was too trashy to have any personal value for our mother. Her daughter was no good either, not having *das echt Blut* running through her genes. Maria did, however, deliver a grandchild quick enough. At seventy-five, it would be our mother's first, and she got a boy. Amniocentesis announced the good news early, and then the boy was induced to spare Mother any inconvenience. He was late, and she had a two-week cruise. Al set it up for Mother that way, and named him Albrecht – Albie – to boot.

The whole time Al was married, Mother loved getting up a list of things for him to do. Dad was never any use that way, and had died in Albie's infancy. When I was back for a rare visit, Mother had Al running all over town. I barely saw him five minutes. She had the money to pay for someone else to do those things, but that wouldn't have occurred to her. She had a son!

When Albie was ten, Maria divorced Al. Things went the usual way, and Maria got the house he'd built for them up in Maine. Al was bitter about the break-up, and month after month wrote 'CUNT' as the payee on the support check stub. At loose ends and working in Massachusetts, he more or less fell back into Mother's orbit. She was at the beach, he stayed in town. Things went on like that for a time, them rubbing each other the wrong way, but staying out of each other's as much as possible.

Things went sidewise the summer Mother turned eighty-seven. Making raspberry jam as she did every summer, she fell and got badly burned. Before, when anything bad happened, she'd always come back stubborn, taking herself where she wanted to go. It didn't work out that way this time. Even though her mind still ticked along well enough, she could no longer live alone. I came back to shepherd her through the various stages of nursing care, close up and sell the winter house, and move her down to the beach permanently. There was no question which child would be taking care of her. She'd chosen Al at his birth.

And so, the second round of them living together full-time started up. It lasted half as long as the first, but was more than twice as bad. Al was never a picnic, and she was as imperious as ever. She'd made him the way she wanted, but she didn't want how he'd turned out. He just wanted her to die.

Al managed the situation with a rough efficiency he might have learned in the Army. Did what was necessary, but there wasn't any affection in it, let alone any love. Mother's progressive descent into senility congealed their relationship into a life sentence shared by prisoner and guard.

I finally begged Al to put her into nursing care when she took to peeing in the street, He wouldn't. Our mother's lifelong frugality was worth millions, and Al was frantic to preserve it for his son: Albie would need custodial care for his entire life.

"She's a useless piece of humanity," Al said one time. "Why can't she just fall down the stairs and break her damn neck?"

With her unerring sense of bad timing, though, he knew she'd never fall right.

I was the only person he could be honest with. I could have gotten leave, gone back more often to give him a break. But I wasn't willing. So, I did one thing right: I listened.

It was a relief when state social services caught wind somehow. They started checking around, then one thing led to another, and our mother went into residential care. I hoped Al could finally have a life of his own.

He seemed happy tinkering, picking up odd jobs, hanging out down at the American Legion Post. Mother was in her nineties by then, and he was still waiting for her to die.

And then she did. But he followed about six weeks later, at fifty-five. The devil's got no reason to visit me now. You have to live with history.

Learning is Born

by Karla Lee Erdman

Wheeling onto the pavement
I slide the gears into park,
turn the ignition off,
and remove the key.

A moment of silence.

The morning wind blows crisply
as I trudge sluggishly
forward toward the door
marked Administration.

The hallway is drowsy,
slow to awaken.
I grab the interoffice mail,
some coffee, too.

As I get closer to my classroom,
I mentally prepare for the
dawning of minds.

At 7:15 a.m. the cacophony of
teenaged voices
announce the marching time.

The bell tolls a five-minute warning.
Some run; others trudge.

All the while
gums flapping
devouring food and conversation.

The clock strikes 7:30.
Recite the Pledge Allegiance.
A moment of silence lasts mere seconds
before important announcements begin.

Within five minutes,
the slam of doors
reverberate down the corridor
count down ninety minutes
until the next bell rings.

Vietnam Vet

by Robert Owen

There is no fanfare, no ticker tape.
Return home through
the underground railroad.
Sneak back in - on your own.
Don't be recognized,
make it seamless - seem less....

What were we fighting for?
Try to make sense of it,
but don't talk to others about it.
They might not understand.
They might not agree
...lucky if you have a job to go to.

Hear a shot, turn to see a Vet fall
on the battlefield, here at home.
Self-inflicted freedom.

Freedom from need
Freedom from want
Freedom from hope
Freedom from despair
Freedom from anguish
Freedom from caring

Freedom - it's what we were fighting for.

Not Apathy. Acceptance.

by Sally K Lehman

It started with a day — maybe these words should be capitalized — A Day. The Day. Four airplanes, two buildings, and thousands of lives later, we live it. We live war — another word that should be capitalized but not by me. That job is way above my pay grade.

Now. Now is relative. Now my kids have become adults. Now I have great nieces and great nephews. Now I have an old woman's spine. Maybe I can capitalize War. Children raised in War. I thought that only happened in other countries: Arab countries, African countries. What a stupid, racist thing to think. White people make War as often as anyone. More so. White people make a business of War. White people make War while thinking in superiority-soaked ways.

Now America is War. We are the occupying force. We have sent people over to other countries to break things and to kill people. Other people. And we can't seem to get out now. That word again. Now.

How much longer? Will my greats and their greats and theirs still be dying from these Now Wars?

I have friends that I didn't know That Day. People who went to the War Zone — another capitalized word. My new friends came home broken in ways I can't always understand. It's easier to understand two lost legs than one lost mind. Knowing these people has changed me. Changed my perspective about War. Made me more invested in community. Given me opinions I didn't have before.

Before. Another word that should have a capital. Before was when our country was safe and our safety was sacrosanct. Before, suburban families looked at big cities and shook their suburban heads. Before, The Bradys were a Bunch, living out the fantasy of a mix and match family, everyone lovey-dovey, no "steps", no lying or cheating that didn't come from children, that wasn't fixable in a single half-hour episode.

Where are our half-hour fixables today?

When did Before end?

Today, we live in After.

After is shoe bombs and no liquids on planes and Ted Kaczynski seems like a minor nuisance of a man, Ted Bundy almost human.

Human. A word I might not capitalize anymore.

Photo by Joe Cantrell

For Vultures: A Dystopia[7]

by Brian Turner

For their hunger, for their patience,
for each circle traced in shadow
and sunk down in the earth
I offer the remorse of flesh,
unflowered and darkening, my life
a gift of heat and steam.

Today, the sun is as high
as the arc of the heavens
will carry it. Let the vultures rise, too.
Let them witness every plume
of smoke, every fallen soldier,
every woman's last kiss
for the ones they love,
and even me when the time comes,
let the vultures feed on me,
let them tear me apart.

---

[7] From *Here, Bullet* - Alice James Books, 2005

The Airplane Graveyard

by Jonathan Oak

It's strange to drive and walk and straighten one's clothes in the presence of death. Breathing seems offensive to the sanctity of death. Eating and laughing and saying hello are heresies. It's not right that I'm not filled every moment with pain and memories. I'm nervous and bored and fidgeting with the radio makes me feel calloused.

Or, they're just distractions to keep me from being overwhelmed. All this watching and analyzing myself, a defense against feeling the things I feel guilty for not feeling.

And then, for an instant, it's on me full force and I can't see or think or feel anything but loss. Then gone again in the distraction of finding a parking space, a space as close to the church front doors as possible so I won't have to walk an extra hundred feet to go look at a dead body.

And that's it.

That's all.

And I'm a jackass.

And when I get inside they'll be waiting in the pews or standing in the foyer. There will be many uncomfortable moments of silence as they shift and glance and blame me with their eyes.

They'll wait till the wake to blame me with their mouths.

His uncle Jacky's smoking outside the front entrance to the church. I stop to have one, too. It takes seven minutes to smoke a cigarette, if you take your time. That's seven minutes that I am not inside.

"Fine day for a funeral, eh, William?"

"Good as any is, Jack."

"Jacky, please."

"Will, please."

I take a moment, looking out across the parking lot, at the snow plowed up in mounds along the road, at the surrounding buildings. Looking everywhere but at Jacky. "Terry's the only one who ever called me William."

"As you like, Will. 'Course, you may be called a lot worse things by the end of the day."

"Mind if I join you?" I ask, pulling a pack from inside my jacket.

Jacky shrugs and makes a thin-lipped face.

It's cold. Smoke and breath blend into great billows in the air above us. A couple of steam engines blowing water and waste into our surroundings to keep us going.

* * *

I got in three days before the funeral. Military transport into Phoenix and half a day's drive before I stopped in Christopher Creek. Had dinner at Creekside Restaurant just before closing. Best fried zucchini anywhere.

Finally pulled into the garage of Terry's little one-bedroom house late, or early, depending on which side of sleep you're on. I brought in my duffel and made tea. Cream and sugar. But just stared at it till it was cold.

At 3:30 in the morning I pulled on my overcoat and stepped into January on the mountaintops of the Mogollon Rim. Snow. Blue snow lit like a stage by the half moon.

I said to the empty world, to Terry's ghost, to the snow and the trees, "I'm here."

The fresh powder flattened the sound and hid the echoes in the layer between earth and ice. Dormant and waiting till spring to whisper out from the edges of receding banks of white. "I'm here. I'm here."

Strike a match, draw and exhale, steam and smoke, and the rustle of fabric, all dead sound. Taken into the dry powder that clung in bunches to pine, was pulled like fresh linen across the ground, tucked in and folded down at the doorstep.

I was freezing in my socks, but I hadn't had the patience for shoes. I just wanted to smoke for a few minutes and think about how quickly things happen. One day you're in Kaiserslautern, then Paris. You're freezing in New York, sweating in Phoenix, then freezing again in Flagstaff, wondering if there's enough gas in the tank to get you all the way up to the Rim.

I dropped the cigarette in the snow. It didn't hiss. It didn't go out. The powder was too cold and dry. So, I snubbed it with my stockinged foot and went inside.

It was too late to keep thinking, so I stripped down to my skin and crawled between cold, fresh linen and waited. Heat gathered into the bed with me. And near the edge of putting it all away till morning I noticed something. Beneath the clean of the freshly made bed there was another scent. His scent, down in the mattress from years of use, come up through the sheets. Disturbed by me, by my crawling into his bed.

My last thought was the two of us lying on each other drunk and laughing. And I didn't notice it then, but I remember it there, head on his pillow, wrapped in the blanket and comforter his mom bought him. His scent.

In his bed, in his house, I guess it was impossible to avoid dreaming of him:

He was younger; maybe twenty-two. Leather jacket, white T-shirt and goofy-grinning, infectious good humor. It looked like my backyard and his backyard and some scene from a movie, like a 70s barbecue in bad color. Everyone was eating hot dogs and hamburgers off bright blue paper plates. Potato salad and baked beans were scooped up with sporks and the ends of potato chips. Red plastic cups of iced and sweetened tea or fruit punch or foaming keg beer.

A B-26 Bomber came flying low over the trees and houses. The Martin Marauder was patched with blue and red over the silver of its body. The propellers were a blur and capped with black cones. It looked straight out of a colorized movie. A badly colorized 1950s plane buzzing over a 1970s colored barbecue.

Me and Terry ran into the house and down into the basement, swinging on the handrails, taking the steps four at a time. The basement/bomb shelter was stocked with beds and food and water. We ran through the rows of beds hollering and laughing and slapping each other on the back with excitement. And I recognized the barracks from Mainz, and I couldn't figure out how Terry had gotten us all the way to Germany without me noticing.

* * *

For the next three days, I was reading. Terry had a small library in his place and one entire bookcase was dedicated to his own writings. There were half-filled notebooks of every size, colored in orange and blue and red, decorated with moons and suns, speckled black and white, bound in cardboard and leather. Some were obviously gifts and others simple spiral Spaldings from the school supply aisle of the local grocery store.

I found one of my favorite stories. I could see where he got the idea from. A little adventure, childhood summers, a bit of romance. As kids the two of us used to play in a junkyard for airplanes. We called it "The Graveyard." It was a good place to hide and tell stories and get tetanus. It's a good thing our parents kept up with our shots. I hear lockjaw is not pleasant and we had plenty of opportunity to acquire it.

I can still see him sitting in the back of the bomber playing tail-gunner and screaming.

"We're hit! We're Hit! There's too many of 'em!"

And we donned imaginary parachutes and jumped from the plane's rusty belly together to explore behind enemy lines. Germany or France. Even remote islands in the Pacific. Sometimes the natives would help us fight the Japanese soldiers who occupied their homes. Sometimes the islanders helped them hunt us instead.

I know how people think these days. Children playing at war. How ludicrous and ugly. But these are the games of children. Games of death, of blood, of adventure. We explored mysterious lands, moved about against our wills by generals, and governments, by politics and survival. It's the classic tale. Make it back home.

"You got a girl in the states?" I'd ask him.

"Yeah. Her name's Linda," which was the name of a girl in our fifth-grade class that Terry had a crush on. "How 'bout you?"

"No. No one special." Which was true.

"Maybe when we get back, then. You know girls like a man in uniform."

"And why's that?" I asked.

"No idea. But whatever works is fine by me."

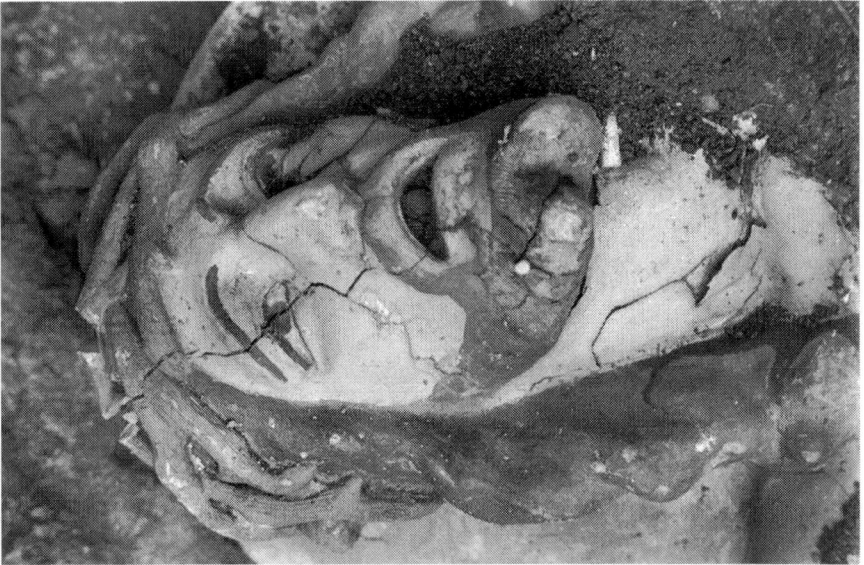

Photo by Joe Cantrell

Inside the chapel it's quiet. The music is soft and inspirational, canned in a factory somewhere in the Southern Baptist Bible Belt. Voices whisper around the hall as family and friends of family talk amid the flowers and plastic, back-lit, "stained glass" windows. The chairs are arranged into rows with an aisle down the middle.

The casket is closed at the front of the room, which makes sense given the letter I'd gotten while boarding the plane home in K-Town. There is a big picture of Terry beside the coffin.

I wonder what his mom would say if she knew I was the one who took it.

I sit in the back, so as not to generate a fuss. Being here is almost as bad as being at Terry's. The loneliness of home, surrounded by familiar sights and people. Only here the people are real, not characters from Terry's stories. Here they can say how I should have been in Show Low with the family that raised me. How I should have stayed with Terry and looked out for him like he looked out for me when we were kids. How I knew he was dangerous by himself, to himself, without someone he trusted. And they'd be right to say it. I'd been saying it for days, blaming myself for not being here.

But he was the one who told me to leave six years ago.

He'd said, "William. I'm a grownup, you know. "

"I know that."

"And I'm older than you."

"I know that, too," I said.

"I know you know that. You finished your Associate's. Been done the last six months. So why are you still here?"

"'Cause I'm s'posed to be."

"Well," he'd said, "s'posed-to-be's not good enough."

* * *

So, I did what we both wanted to do and I got out, the easiest way we knew how. Through an airplane graveyard. But instead of a Pacific island, or the Middle East, I was assigned to an Army Air Force facility in Germany and was a mechanic for six years.

I spent every chance I had in a different country.

I got Terry to join me on leave in France once, and we went together to the Lascaux caves. It was part of our, "If ever I before I die" list. Some of the oldest cave paintings in the world are there. Twenty-thousand years waiting in the dark. The Hall of Bulls was a wonder of ochre pigments, red and yellow and brown. The largest bull was three times the height of a man. It was nothing like the pictures I'd seen. He was vital and frightening. An early god who'd slept so long he could no longer wake.

"Here we go," Terry said. He took my flashlight from me and pointed both his and mine up under his chin. He smiled broadly and his eyes went big just before he shut them both off.

And it was dark, like fairy tales before people worried about screwing up their children. There's nothing for the eye to latch on to, no glimmer or grey, just the images in your head leaping across the paisley stars and the rolling colors of eyes deprived. Images of tree lines and women hanging clothes. Thought becomes sight, becomes cars moving and faces smiling, monsters yawning sorrow and books closing. So detailed and solid come the flashes that you have to wonder if you're peeking in through gaps between seconds, wonder if the dark has stopped time or made it stutter around you. Light keeps time. Light grounds you in the present, in a place.

There were bulls and horses blinking in the black. There were stags and bears shaking their heads to clear them. There were cats and bison flowing on the walls around us. Without the light, they were breathing again. They were dreaming again. Remembering rather than being remembered.

"Terry? Terry?"

"I'm here."

"Gimme your hand."

I heard the smile in his voice when he said, "Okay." He was laughing at me. He was smiling in the dark. Expressions useless. The blind imagining the blind.

"Why are we doing this?"

"Because this is the end, man. Buried in night. Eventually we all have to grow accustomed to it."

respect your mother

by Antonia Benson

Separation of the nations
    why are we letting our differences
    be run by hate &
       comparison?

Acting like it's all a game.
as if a shot to the face won't remain
    & you'll wake up in 30 seconds
       to a ring and
       a voice saying
         'new game, new game.'
You only live once
why are weapons our choice to defend
          what we love?
    A backwards world
    it's a negative swirl,
  if you deny your differences
      you'll be sucked into the whirl.

Whirlwind of pleasing others
& not respecting your mother.
What she has taught
      is natural.
A force of unconditional
      love
that we deny
because of the hatred passing by.

You'll never crawl out of the hole
if you,
    yourself,
      don't feel whole.

Fifty Caliber Machine Gun

by Jacob Meeks

December 2002 – A Mountain in Afghanistan on the Pakistani Border

"Huff!" I heard Sergeant Hearns yell. "Get the fuck out here!"

I wondered what the shit was going on. I hadn't even woken up yet.

Billy rushed in the old Russian shack. "Man, you better get out here. Shit's getting real," Billy said.

Goddammit. I sprung up, grabbed my weapon and ran outside.

I saw Sergeant Hearns standing on the edge of the hill. He pointed down towards the base camp.

"You see that shit?"

I nodded my head.

"Get on the gun," Hearns said.

I sat down on my ass, knees up and looked down the barrel of the fifty-cal. On the far-left side of the compound in the valley below us, a white van had pulled up. Ten men, all armed, came out and scattered around the back side of the compound. I figured the distance was around 1200 meters. I could pin the three at the van easy. No problem. The others were on the back side of the compound, meaning I'd have to lob rounds over the compound itself. Way too dangerous. But I could get the first three.

We watched the Afghans for a second. Were they really trying to attack this compound? It didn't make any sense. It wasn't my problem.

"You got a shot?" Hearns asked.

"Roger," I replied. Silence.

I stared down the barrel of the gun. Time slowed down. Sweat dripped down my brow. I wondered if I was going to have to take these men's lives. Something chemical in my brain shifted. It was like some kind of biological wire in my brain snapped.

This is real, I thought. I can kill. I can take another human being's life.

I didn't have any time to consider the moral implications of the moment. If I can kill, what does that make me? Man's the only creature on Earth that seems to consider the killing they do, other creatures just do it because they're wired that way. It's natural. Is it natural for us? Are we just animals? Something worse? Something better?

Too much time passed, even though it had only been a minute. It didn't look like these guys were attacking.

Not my call.

I looked up at Sergeant Hearns and asked, "Hey boss, you want me to shoot these motherfuckers?"

Hearns looked down at me and said, "Nah dawg. We might have to explain that shit later."

Another minute passed and the Afghan soldiers got back in their van and went on their merry way. I unloaded the gun.

We got a radio call a few minutes later. Apparently, these were AMF forces, friendly to us and the Special Forces guys in the camp.

Apparently, they were just messing with the SF. It might have been nice if someone had told us.

I spent the next seven months in the gun turret of a Hum-V sitting with my thumbs on the trigger of a fifty-caliber machine gun, one of the most brutally effective weapons on the face of the planet. I was once told that a bullet from a fifty-cal could go by somebody's arm and, if it was close enough, it would take the entire arm off from the sheer force of pressure. Luckily, I never had to see if that was true or not. I went through those seven months and never had to pull the trigger on another human being. I got lucky.

Sometimes shit happens. Sometimes it don't. I was happy when we left Afghanistan. I smiled to myself. I thought this has been a good deployment. I didn't have to kill anyone. I had been sitting on a machinegun this whole time and it was my responsibility to kill if needed. And I learned that I could kill, that I was capable, for whatever that meant. But it didn't happen. I felt relieved. I might be a US Army, Infantry, Airborne soldier, but I had no desire to kill anyone. No desire at all. I just wanted to go home and try to have a life like everyone else.

Leaving the Army and coming home was strange. The Army had been my life for four years. It had been my identity. In many ways, I had become institutionalized. I was used to being around my fellow soldiers. I was used to being able to talk about things and everyone around me would understand. When I got out of the Army, that all just disappeared.

I tried to talk to people. I tried to explain things to them. I tried to tell them stories. I failed. I couldn't put my experiences in context. Listeners would always want to hear about certain things. One of the most common questions I received after people found out I was in the military was, have you ever killed anyone?

I hated the question. I hated people for asking that question. The first time I heard it, I couldn't believe the person was asking. I was just stunned and I walked away. The second time, and many times after that, I got angry. I would yell and tell them how stupid they were for asking that question. Later on, I started to think it was a trick question. If you answered yes then you would suddenly be judged to be crazy and not part of normal society. If you answered no, then suddenly you had not been through anything in the military or felt anything. I never tried to brag about my service. I never would. I find that insulting to all the other men and women who served. It was still part of me though and I wanted, needed, to talk about it. When I did, I felt judgment. For a short time, civilians almost made me feel guilty for being so happy that I never had to pull the trigger.

We watch movies and television and see hundreds of disposable bad guys get shot, and we think nothing of it. I think our minds start to transpose life with mindless entertainment and mindless entertainment with life. We start to think that life is like those movies. Deep down, we know it's not. Deep down, there's a part of us that still realizes real life is a biological, chemical soup that's a mixture of senses and emotions like fear and anger and that nothing is so simple.

We have a lot of ways to cover up that part of our nature but it doesn't mean it's not still there.

The day that I learned I could kill stuck with me for a long time. It influenced me in ways that I did not know. I had been in a car wreck after coming home that damaged my body. As I was healing, I would walk around like a wounded dog that got backed into a corner. If anyone got too close, I would bite. The wire in my mind that had snapped made me much quicker to anger. It made me want to escalate things quickly. I had anxiety. I had bad dreams. I kept to myself.

I've come to think it's not the capability to take life that defines a person, but rather the choices they make with that capability. Of course, I also know that sometimes you don't have choice. The universe is a crap shoot.

I know that life isn't a movie. I think that in our modern, media driven world the majority of our brains can't understand what it might mean to someone to really take a life. I think we're scared that, if someone else we consider moral and normal can do it, then is it possible that we ourselves can take life? What does that make us then? Who are we? What the hell is right and wrong?

I don't know the answer to those questions. It's heavy shit. I do know that I have a responsibility to try and live a moral life. I know that I cannot shape nature but I can respect it and try to live in harmony with it, while maintaining some kind of human morality.

I know that something changed for me that day on that mountaintop behind that fifty-caliber machine gun.

COHORT OF MIST, FOG AND FIRE[8]

by M.F. McAuliffe

(Hawthorne, CA, 1983)

wadewalk the thick
black
cold
hellroar
oh god move! phosphorus
burn
ing meatmist

The mist would lie all along the trees in the mornings. Anything could be inside there, in the shadows and the dark. You were out in the open.

The only thing to do was keep moving. Mortar takes out two, three guys at once.

So you keep moving and watching, praying the goddam mist will burn off.

For a while after I came back I'd wake up, rigid with terror, sweating, drenched in sweat; I'd just lie there, paralyzed.

---

[8] Previously published in The Gravity of the Thing

boom

ing

burn

I never could sleep. Even at my grandmother's house I'd wake up in the middle of the night and lie there awake while the floorboards creaked.

*****

I get here at five, five-fifteen. That early the fog just swallows the campus.

I go to my room and get stuff ready to duplicate, Aristotle, an essay on Cause, maybe, or Effect, then an essay on Cause and Effect.

We start the Literature section with morality in fiction. I ask the kids about their lives and then we do the tragedies, Oedipus, Antigone. After class I do a little tutoring, work out extra reading for the really bright kids. If a kid is failing I'll go visit the family and find out what the problem is.

*****

The great thing is to take it as it comes. Keep your dignity. Keep your integrity.

The Army's the greatest teacher in the world. There's only one answer for any question and you learn that answer because your life depends on it.

★★★

I used to dance a lot, hit the clubs. I loved dancing. But I haven't been able since I got back. Too much surgery. My wife likes to go out to dinner, so we go out pretty much every night. After that I read till one, two, sleep a little and then come in to school.

★★★

That early, the fog just swallows the campus. Sometimes around the middle of the day the sun starts to burn through, this greyed and flailing thing twitching in the last of the fog, trapped up there, dim and pitted and guttering. It's nothing. It's just a ghost hanging there, half the colour of the moon.

Fifteen Ways to Say Peace[9]

- ❖ **Cherokee:** ᎦᏙᎯ (dohiyi)
- ❖ **Welsh:** heddwch
- ❖ **Irish:** Síocháin
- ❖ **Basque:** Baké
- ❖ **Italian:** Pace
- ❖ **Dutch:** Vrede
- ❖ **Japanese:** 平和 *(heiwa)*
- ❖ **Arabic:** سلام *(salām)*
- ❖ **Bulgarian:** Мир *(mir)*
- ❖ **Tibetan:** ཞི་བདེ *(zhi-bde)*
- ❖ **Danish:** Fred
- ❖ **Greek:** Ειρήνη *(iríni)*
- ❖ **Persian/Farsi:** صلح *(solh)*
- ❖ **Hindi:** शांति *(śānti)*
- ❖ **Thai:** สันติภาพ *(santipap)*

---

[9] http://www.k-international.com/blog/international-peace-day-how-to-say-peace-in-35-languages/

Photo by Joe Cantrell

Arnold Duplantier 3rd

by Damon Hugh Faust

It was late June 2005. I sat in Baghdad International Airport looking through the Army Times. I was waiting for my Chinook back to forward operating base Falcon, better known as FOB Falcon, or better yet, as home. I went straight to the death/wounded listing at the back of the paper. This was my metric of how the war/conflict/operation/ whatever-you-want-to-call-it was going this week.

19 KIA.

40 WIA.

Ok, ok, not bad.

Then there was this intense, very fucked up conversation I had with myself while looking at the casualty totals: The dead and wounded mean this is a real war, right? One my step-dad (a Vietnam Vet) could be proud of.

My step-dad was out of my life by age seven. Later on, I found out he had attempted suicide three times, struggled with substance abuse, and suffered from PTSD, so who's to say how he would have judged me? But to me he was still the warrior my seven-year-old-self idolized, and I constantly compared myself to him. His war stories, his box of medals, that warrior I had created in my very young mind. After each patrol, each contact or IED blast, every time, I checked the Army Times casualty listing. Comparing my war to his. And by my accounts we are looking good, while KIA's aren't even close, our wounded in action is off the charts—

WAIT....

Arnold Duplantier 3rd
     Arnold Duplantier 3rd
     Arnold....

My eyes began to blur.

Was Dup a 3rd??? Nah, this must be a mistake.

"Hey, does this say Arnold Duplantier 3rd?" I asked the soldier sitting next to me, who was clearly trying to take a nap and had no time for whatever I was saying.

"Yeah," a quick one-word response.

"Fuck, that's my guy. That's my guy, can that be right?"

"Yeah, man, that's what it says." A few more words this time from the napping soldier, who went right back to his nap.

I frantically looked for José in the airport, knowing he was in-route home as well. José was our company medic and my closest friend. I didn't find him until were boarding our Chinook. It was my deepest desire that he would tell me it wasn't true, that Dup was still alive. He, however, confirmed my fear. Dup was gone. Shot through the small spaces in his protective vest under the armpit and neck by a Chechen sniper.

"Sniper?" I asked, confused by two facts. "When did snipers get to our little corner of the war? What the fuck? Chechen? Where, what, who is a Chechen sniper?"

"Yeah, there are two, maybe three in our sector. They got Dup at the community council meeting, he was on the roof pulling security. They also got Carpenter in the neck but Doc Archie saved his life, treated him and pulled him to cover." José always had the latest info and delivered it with accuracy like the professional he was.

"Fuck, bro...it just got real," I said.

Nothing else was said between us. We knew it was time to work. It was time for us to be the rocks of Charlie Rock, our company. The guys who lived through this moment would need us and our steadfast resolve now more than ever. We were the fortunate ones. We would carry this for them. We would cover down.

VIOLENCE THROUGH SPEED AND AUDACITY- Charlie Rock's motto.

Time to work.

You typically had twenty-four hours to re-acclimate after leave. However, upon returning to the platoon the tempo was high, and within two hours I found myself behind the wheel of my Humvee leading our three-Humvee section outside the wire.

We didn't talk about Dup for some time, we just put in work. I found myself volunteering for as many patrols and missions as I could, opting out of the 12 to 24-hour rest cycles built into our operations.

It was on one of those patrols after the anger of losing Dup had subsided that acceptance kicked in.

Acceptance that I'd never play spades with Dup again.

Acceptance that this was a real war.

Acceptance that this was my war.

Acceptance I would die here, in the cradle of civilization.

This acceptance lead to a heavy chest; a chest full of medals.

Our section saw the smoke before we hit the main road, Route Irish. Lt. Fox radioed back to HQ that we had what appeared to be a house fire and we were responding.

We crossed the three to four lanes of the Route Irish, jumped the railroad tracks to the frontage road, and put our three-Humvee patrol in security positions.

Without thought for myself and wanting death, craving its release, I jumped out of the Humvee with our small fire extinguisher and entered the three-story building, which was ablaze.

Once entering the threshold, I was met by an Iraqi who directed me into the home. I noticed quickly the entryway was full of propane tanks, the whole first floor for that matter, and as I fought the fire the best I could, the same Iraqi emerged from the smoke with a small Iraqi boy. We quickly got the boy out and Doc Murilo began to work on him, his charred bright pink flesh blinding out the sun.

Myself and the Iraqi returned to the building, empty extinguisher in hand, to pull out an elderly Iraqi woman who was bloated and disfigured from the flames and smoke.

I knew this house of death was where I belonged and if not here, I would find another house of death to make my bed.

To someone who hurt me:

by Kat Altair

Jones -

First of all, you are a bastard. An asshole. Actually, I can only remember your name with profanity, and not remember you at all. You aren't worth the time or energy of a letter or any attention for that matter. Even though you are the name at the top of this letter and part of it, you are not the only part of the story- you aren't that important. You just happened to be where it started.

Those who attack others have a certain amount of power, but it is not as you would believe, particularly as you didn't even have the power to attack me without help. Attackers would like to believe that they conquered, but you could not without allies. Abusers, assaulters, and attackers would like to believe that you have the right to hold a certain place in the memory of those you abuse, assault, and attack.

No. The power of those who attack and abuse is in the memory of the incident, not the person. The memory that experiencing trauma leaves behind. The memory you left behind.

Whether or not I think about it, there will always be the experience of the assault you and your "friends" carried out against me. To top it off, you then did something which would lead to far more damage- more trauma than the attack itself. You lied. You lied to cover your own ass for raping me with your buddies to begin with. You told my CO, our CO, that I was gay- a fact you could not have truthfully known at the time. You cost me my rank, my sanity, and ultimately my career.

You were the reason my room would be raided several nights a week for a year. You were the reason I experienced solitary confinement (imposed on me through rules which kept me away from my peers) away from my job, required others to see me as a pariah not to be interacted with, why I was fucked with for a year by my whole unit. All of which are experiences no one should have to go through, let alone going through it just because of who you are attracted to.

You *villainized* me. And for what? Because I wouldn't sleep with you? Because I hurt your precious, baby 18-year-old pride? Your actions are the reason I was denied promotion and was denied by the med board. I spent weeks fighting in Washington D.C. with a JAG lawyer from hell, and you are the reason I was ultimately discharged. It all started with you.

You led my beloved Marine Corps in a crusade against me. You. Someone I would have gladly given my life for because we shared the same uniform. A betrayal I would not have anticipated from someone I would die for. You and your buddies. You could have done almost anything else to me and I still would have taken a bullet for you. But you cost me my uniform. You cost me my identity.

Even now, almost ten years later, the things you caused and did to me continue to plague me like cancer cells that spread throughout my life. Every time I think it's taken care of, a new tumor pops up, sometimes in a new place and sometimes in a place it has been before. This often means more excruciating "treatment" I have to go through, on top of the previous impact made in every other aspect of my life and family.

You may have started this, but you no longer hold the title of this pain. You probably hold pride in "manning up" to rape me but understand this, you as an individual mean nothing to me.

The title of my pain now is the "assault and investigation." The power you hold now is only in being remembered for starting it all, but you aren't who or what I think about every day. Even when I do think about the day you and your buddies raped me, your face is not the only one I remember. The look in your eyes isn't the only one I see in the dark. You are just a small piece of it all.

At some point, I honestly hope all of you experience even a portion of the hell you caused me. For starters, you should try being in solitary for even a week and see how it treats you. Regardless, I won't think about you enough to know. I won't look you up online. I won't ask people we served with how you are. I can hope you suffer, but I won't give you the time of day to even be curious.

Sincerely hoping you die a painful death alone,
Altair

✱✱✱

Their response:

Altair,

It's weird to hear from you after all these years. Was Ft. Leonard Wood really ten years ago? I talked to Farmer the other day, he sounds good. I haven't heard from SSgt. Hazel in a while though, do you know how he's doing? If you hear from him, have him give me a call.

Look, I know you're mad about what happened but really, you deserved it. You were the only female in the unit. It's not like I thought you would remember it, anyway.

Besides, better me than Roberts, he's the one that wanted to in the first place. He would always say that women Marines- WM- are each a "Walking Mattress" since that's what it stands for. He said you didn't have the right to turn me down. Besides, I was easier than he was going to be. He would have done it, too, if Farmer hadn't come out and "saved" you.

Does it really matter that you got investigated anyway? I mean...you *are* gay. You should have known you would get found out. You knew the rules when you enlisted, after all, and it's not my fault you're a fag. Roberts said we would "turn you straight." I'm sorry we didn't, we could have saved you from getting discharged.

Just remember, it could have been worse.

Anyway, I'll talk to Farmer, see if he's heard from SSgt. We should all meet somewhere and have a weekend together so we can drink and catch up. You could bring your girl, wife, whatever. We could have fun with her, too.

Jones

Garden of Scars

by Ryan Holleran

A constellation of pocked scars
stares down at us from the T-walls
as we stroll to dinner.
Evidence of the rockets
so quick to mark the land,
much slower to mark me.
My life left to hang in its own
constellation of violence.

Ba-Boom!

Ba, the sound of the rocket finding the ground.
Boom, the sound of the charge detonating

Its arrival preceded by a whistle.

I was grateful at the time for the warning,
this high-pitched scream that would
haunt me forever after.
Could I outrun a rocket?
Would I be running to meet it
and my grave?

47 holes,
craters,
wounds that mark the earth.
How brutality marks my life.
Marked by a geyser of dust.

47 flowers of death
bolting outside the East gate,
our base becoming a

garden of scars,
carbon copies of ourselves.

Where were these rockets just minutes before?
From whose home were they fired?
A home like any I have known—
abundant with the love of family.
Rockets fired in a desperate act of
love *for* family!

Their homes, like ours
left to reflect
the brutal design of war.

A Poem About the Way Things Are Sometimes

by Julie Elefante

My father still sharpens my mother's knives by hand.
The blades initially resist,
reverberate their say in the patience of the conversation
between his fingers and the whetstone,
hissing violently for long minutes at first
until they're lulled into a hush,
the peak of their lethality pointed
into whispers just shy of forgiveness.

My Father's Other Wars

by Julie Elefante

After the U.S. declared war against Iraq back in 2003, I was talking to my dad on the phone and asked him what he thought about the war.

He said, "War? I've had enough of war."

I'd seen photos of him in Vietnam where he served as a member of the U.S. Navy, but I didn't realize the scope of that statement at the time.

It's rare anymore that I get to spend some alone time with my dad. Inevitably, when I do, he tells me a story. Here's the last story he told me back in 2014 during my Thanksgiving visit while my mom and brother were tackling a morning of Black Friday shopping. We were watching Ghost Hunters, and he asked me if I believed in ghosts. I told him I did, and I mirrored the question. He said he did, too. He told me about a path he'd have to walk to and from his village near Santiago at night. Along the path was a giant tree he'd have to walk under, and every time he had to walk under this tree, he'd get the worst chills. One night, just as he walked under the tree, hundreds of bats who'd been hanging in the tree took flight, and, terrified, he ran all the way back to his village.

Then he told me the story of why he had to walk the path at night.

During World War II, all the men in the village were expected to take a night shift, watching for Japanese boats that would land on the beach where his village sat, right on the water. Because the men worked hard all day, they were allowed to have their teenage sons take their shifts. So, while the rest of the villagers hid in the mountain jungle above the village, the night watcher would hide on the beach to keep an eye out.

One night, when my sixteen-year-old dad was walking down the path to the beach to tend to his watch, he heard yelling coming from the sea. He hadn't even noticed the Japanese boats bobbing in the surf. Scrambling to hide, he watched the Japanese soldiers point their boats toward the village he'd been heading for. As he watched, they swarmed the beach, and they set fire to all the huts in the village.

My dad listed them off, going down the row of homes in his head, saying family names of cousins I'd grown up with, adding his own family's hut to the list, all the way through the tiny village. After the village was entirely ablaze, he watched as they burned the sugar cane fields beyond the village, the fire spreading, destroying everything. And it burned all the way to the town of Santiago miles away, burning his church to the ground and blazing on into the town.

There was a breath-long silence, just long enough for a phantom to fill his chest.

And then my dad said it was because they saw him.

"What do you mean?" I asked.

"They saw me, so they burned my village down."

"How could they have seen you at night?"

"The moon was out, and the whole shore was lit up."

"No. That wasn't your fault."

"You don't think so?"

"No."

"I think it was."

"You're wrong." Stupid, pointless words.

There have been a handful of times when I've wished I could rewrite history or brought down the mercy of the cosmos with a simple utterance, and, in each of those times, the impotence of those words has seeded itself into my marrow. But plugged into life's lens, perspective is a bittersweet blessing.

Coming Home Again

by William Bradford Nichols

Chris stares at his phone. Two missed calls. One text. All from Holly. "Miss u. Hope you're having a good night. Call me soon please."

He takes a long, slow pull from the Jamieson that is slowly melting the ice in his coffee cup. He looks at the phone a little longer before setting it on the table next to the commemorative M911A1 .45 ACP he had ordered on his way out of Iraq. It is nickel plated with an inlaid pearl grip, etched with the symbol of the All-Americans on one side and parachute wings on the other. On the barrel is an etching of the country of Iraq on one side, and the dates Jan '08'- Jan '09' on the other.

He picks up the profile the doctor had printed out for him. Post-Traumatic Stress Disorder and Major Depressive Disorder, it says. He keeps reading. Must be allowed eight hours of sleep every day, it says. No weapons, no ammo, no shooting or qualification ranges, it says. No combat simulation training exercises, no alcohol use; the list goes on and on. The doctor had asked if he wanted to hurt himself or others.

"No," he'd said.

The doctor had asked if he had any weapons in the house.

"No," he had said again.

"I'm going to have to call your chain of command and let them know. They'll probably want to check your house. They're going to have to make sure you don't have any guns."

"That's fine," he'd said. "They know me. I'm not going to hurt anybody. I already told you, I got rid of all my guns. They can come over whenever they want, but we're off for the day. I can give you my Platoon Sergeant's personal number if you want it."

"No need," she'd said. "It's all in your intake paperwork."

"Right," he'd said.

"How's the Prozac working?" the doctor had asked.

"Good, I think."

"Ok," she'd said. "And how's your sleep?"

He had wanted to say, *I wake my wife up four or five times every night asking her if she heard what I just heard. I jump up every time she moves and ask her what's going on. Or worse, I jump up and run around the house like a fucking mad man trying to find the person I heard break in. I hear explosions. I hear people run up the stairs. I hear people open the doors to my kids' rooms and I know they're going to hurt them.*

He'd wanted to tell her about the constant nightmares. The screams. The smell of burning. The hot, coppery smell of blood. He could only say so much, though. He had just wanted the diagnosis, not a stay in the hospital.

"Fine," he'd said. "My sleep is fine."

It had been a fine fucking line he'd had to walk. Saying just enough for them to be concerned but not enough to make them admit him. Chris had already made up his mind, but he needed that PTSD diagnosis. She had said he couldn't get it for six months. So, he took his temporary diagnosis of Adjustment Disorder and went back once a week. Now, he finally has the diagnosis in hand. He has the paper.

The diagnosis is in his record. A couple of his friends had already suck started their fucking carbines, and he had found out that as long as they had a PTSD diagnosis, the life insurance would still pay out. He thinks it is enough. Enough for Holly to buy a house and pay for college for the three kids. The Army insurance isn't enough by itself, but he was smart enough to take out a shit-ton before both of his deployments. When he got back this time, he just never turned it off.

He is not scared. He is...relieved.

Chris has known something for a long time now. In short, he knows that he will pay for his sins. He doesn't believe in karma or any of that shit.

This is real.

This is truth.

Worse yet, he doesn't necessarily believe that he will be the one to pay. He has become ever increasingly certain that it is his children who will pay the price for the shit he did in Iraq. Maybe they will get hit by a car. Maybe they will be kidnapped. Raped. Tortured. Murdered. Cancer. Maybe there will be a wreck and they will burn alive.

Like she did.

He takes a long deep swig of his whiskey. It burns in his throat. He closes his eyes and sees her immediately.

★★★

She is slumped in the back of the car. She is burning.

"Come on! Get in there, Doc!" It's Smoke. Has to be.

Chris turns to look at him. Flames are reflecting off his ballistic eye protection. He is smiling.

"Help 'em, Doc. The fuck are you waiting for?" Killings, has to be.

"Shut the fuck up," Chris says.

Killings laughs.

"Come on, Doc, ain't this your fucking job?"

"Fuck no it isn't," Chris says. "My job is to save your dumb ass, not these motherfuckers," Chris says as he nods his head in the direction of the conflagration that used to be a car. That used to be a family.

"All right, get back from there, Doc," Smoke says.

Chris doesn't move. He stares at the burning car.

"Get back, Doc," Smoke says again.

Chris turns quickly and his face is changed. His eyes are wide, desperate, wild. His jaw is slack, his face is pale and emblazoned with a look of abject horror.

"Where's the fire extinguisher?!" Chris yells.

"What?" Smoke asks.

"She's moving. She's fucking moving!" Chris screams. He is frantic. Smoke runs at him and grabs Chris, right as he starts to run towards the rear gun truck.

"What the fuck? Let go of me!" Chris yells.

"Just calm the fuck down," Smoke says. "That vehicle was burning for twenty minutes before we even got here; there's no fucking way that little girl is moving!"

"I got him, Smoke," Killings says. Killings grabs him by the shoulders and begins subtly maneuvering him away.

"He's your soldier, Sergeant," Smoke says. "Get his ass under control." Smoke looks behind Chris, towards the trucks. "Are you ready for a briefing, Sir?" Smoke asks.

"Are you ready to give one?" a gruff voice responds. Lieutenant Meyerson, has to be.

"Yes Sir," Smoke says. They move towards the burning car. Chris can hear their conversation as they leave.

"What the hell is wrong with Doc?" Meyerson asks.

Chris isn't able to hear Smoke's response.

"The fuck, man?" asks Killings. "You good, bro?"

"Yeah," Chris says. "I'm good now. I just...Jesus Christ, I thought she was moving, man." His voice breaks as he tries to stifle the words in his throat. "I thought she was moving," he says again. He looks away, not wanting Killings to see the tears brimming in his eyes.

***

He opens his eyes. He is crying now. He looks at the .45 on the table. The phone next to it vibrates abruptly. Chris startles and spills his drink.

"God fucking damn it!" screams Chris. "I am so fucking tired of this bullshit!"

He throws the glass at the wall and reaches for the gun. The phone vibrates again, rhythmically. She is calling again. He stares at it for a few agonizing seconds, waiting for the phone's spasmodic seizure to stop. He should answer. He wants to answer, but he knows if he does, he might lose his nerve.

Fuck that, he thinks. *Mercy is for the weak and I don't fucking deserve any. This shit ends now.*

He reaches for the .45 on the table. A bell-tone sounds, signaling a text. He grabs his phone instead.

"You have two seconds to call me before I call Janice and tell her to check on you."

Janice lives next door and could literally walk here in seconds. He wants to do this shit, but he doesn't want to do it with that fucking dependapotamus banging on his front door. The phone vibrates again in his hand.

"Fuck it," he says and pushes the digital green phone that is flashing on his screen, slides it to the right, and then sticks the phone to his ear.

He cannot speak.

"Honey? Are you there?" Holly asks.

After a few seconds, he tries to talk. His voice cracks immediately. He swallows hard, takes a deep breath, and tries again.

"Yeah, babe, I'm here. What's up?" *Is that convincing?* He hopes it is.

"Are you ok? What's going on? Why didn't you answer my texts and phone calls?"

"I was uh...I fell asleep...on the couch for a little bit and I forgot to take my phone off vibrate after final formation earlier."

That is a lie. He wasn't there. He has to get off the phone now, before she suspects anything.

"Have you been drinking?" Holly asks.

Damn it, he thinks. *Am I slurring?*

No. He is not slurring. He hasn't drunk that much. Not as much as usual. He's too afraid he'll pass out if he drinks too much. Afraid that if he does pass out, his mind will have changed by the time he wakes up. No, it isn't the alcohol she is hearing. It is his fucking crying, his desperation, his sadness. It is his weakness.

I have to get off the phone, he thinks again. *Now.*

"A little, babe. I'm not drunk if that's what you're asking."

"Are you alone?"

"Yeah. Why?"

"Why are you drinking alone?"

"I don't drink to get drunk, babe. I just drink so I can calm down; you know that," he says.

I just drink so I can fucking sleep at night, is what he wants to say.

"What's going on honey?"

"Nothing," he says. "I'm just tired. Rough week. I should go to bed, babe. Can I call you in the morning?"

"Okay," she says reluctantly.

Thank God, Chris thinks. *She's buying it. Jesus, I have to get off the phone before she figures something out.*

He begins to wonder why he even answered the phone. He could have pulled the trigger long before Janice had gotten her fat ass off her couch and made her way to his front door. The thought enters his mind that this is the last time they will ever talk. For a moment, the realization of how much guilt Holly is going to feel come morning crashes through his head, but he immediately pushes it far away. She will never feel as bad about this as she will if one, or all, of the kids get hurt because he doesn't have the balls to take care of his own shit.

Honestly, he thinks, *It's the best thing for her, too. Who wants to have to live with someone that is this fucked up for the rest of their lives? Holly deserves a life with someone who acts like a fucking human being. Not someone who drags her under the bed in the middle of the night because he thinks he hears intruders, or rockets. Not someone who she had to ask to get rid of his guns because he woke up one night and ran around clearing every room in the house with a loaded 12-guage looking for burglars. Not someone whose very existence threatens the lives of her children.*

Chris takes a deep breath.

"You know I love you, hon, right?"

"What?" she asks.

"I know things have been really bad since I got back. I want you to know that I love you. You and the kids, and I'm sorry." His voice cracks again as he says that last part.

Through the phone, he can hear her start to whimper. She cries. Chris takes another deep breath, swallows, and chokes back his own tears.

"I've got to go, babe."

"Ok," she says, endeavoring to hold back her own tears.

He waited a second.

"I'll call you in the morning, Holly. Sleep good, ok?"

He can tell she is gaining control of herself again. This is another reason, he is so tired of hurting her. Yelling at the kids for no reason. Screaming at her. Apologizing. Screaming again. They will be sad at first, but he knows that, in the end, they'll be just as relieved as he is. Relieved not to have to put up with any more of his shit.

"I love you, Holly."

Holly says nothing.

Oh, shit.

He wasn't thinking when he'd spoken. Wasn't guarding. Wasn't controlling. He had fucked up. She still knows him. She still knows his voice. She can still tell when he is lying.

Damn it, he thinks. *What a stupid fucking mistake.*

"Chris, babe," says Holly. Her voice has changed. She has switched to mom mode. She is going to get to the bottom of this shit. "What are you doing right now?"

"Nothing, babe. Don't be so paranoid. I really need to go to bed, Holly."

"No," she says. "Talk to me for a second. What are you doing? What are you thinking about, hon?"

The whole thing rushes through his head again: PTSD, life insurance, lots of fucking money. She can buy a house, pay for colleges, pay for weddings. Most importantly, none of the kids will have to pay for the shit their dad did in Iraq. It is right. It makes sense. She will understand.

I can make her understand, he thinks. *She will see that this is the right thing to do.*

"I'm thinking I'm gonna kill myself, Holly. I got my PTSD diagnosis today. That means the insurance will still pay out and you guys will have enough money for everything you need." He waits, listens. No breathing. Nothing. Not a sound. "Babe? Babe, I really need to go, OK?"

"Chris," she says. "Chris, honey, listen to me, ok?" Her voice is calm, measured. It is not strained, it is controlled. "That's a bad idea OK? A really bad idea."

"What?" he asks. *What the fuck is she talking about*, he thinks, *how is this a bad idea?* "Why? What do you mean?" Chris asks. *She isn't getting it. I'm not explaining it right.*

"We love you, Chris," she says with trembling voice. In his mind, he can see the look of shock on her face. "I love you. The kids love you. We'll help you through anything, honey, but you have to stay alive. We love you, Chris. We love you so much." She's crying again.

"Did you forget about Killings?" she asks. "Lavinia found him. She was five years old, Chris. That family is ruined." She is near shouting now. Before her anger has a chance to overtake her, her voice cracks and she begins sobbing into the phone.

Now he remembers what her crying reminds him of. Jessica, Killings's wife. And his kids. The only place he had heard crying like that before Killings's funeral was in Iraq.

Like clockwork, his thoughts return to the car, and the girl.

Two women had come out of one of the nearby buildings and were on their knees wailing when Chris and the rest of 3rd Platoon arrived. Their 'terp told them that they were the mother and grandmother of the child in the car. The wife and mother of the man. The sounds they made are haunting.

It is the sound Missy, Jessica, and the children made at Killings's funeral.

It is the sound his wife is making now.

It is a sound he had never wanted to hear again.

Chris realizes almost instantly that what she is saying is true. He had justified Killings's suicide.

He had understood it.

He had even begun to think that it was right, noble. He sees now that it isn't true. Killings is just gone. He is dead. His family's souls died with him.

They had lived through so much shit together. Two tours in Iraq, firefights, IED's, rocket attacks. All of that for him to die in his own bed, by his own hand.

Chris is crying now.

For almost a full year he has thought about nothing, except for this one thing, every goddamned day. Jesus Christ.

"We love you, Chris. We love you so much," she says. She is repeating it like a mantra. "You're a good father. You're a good husband. I love you. Please don't do this, Chris. Please don't leave us. Please don't leave us."

The doorbell rings: three quick bursts. *Janice,* he thinks, as he rises and moves towards the entryway.

On the phone, he can still hear Holly crying.

Death of Rainbow
by Sean Davis

Charlie stands with a fake solemnity over the toilet in his two-bedroom, one-bath apartment with a dead betta fish in the palm of his hand. His five-year-old son beside him, sobbing. The boy's chest heaving, but standing with his head down. This interests Charlie when most things do not anymore. Usually when the little guy falls apart like this, he collapses on the floor in a heap or runs to his bed. Charlie takes the fact that he isn't in the fetal position as progress in his emotional development. Charlie breathes in to say something, but nothing comes.

The boy's eyes start up toward Charlie's hand and at Rainbow the fish, but then drop back down like the emotion they carry is too heavy. The tears flow in two steady streams over the red, full cheeks and the ones that aren't sucked in by his flared nostrils drip from his chin.

***

The Battle of Najaf, July of 2004, Charlie's squad has been fighting for six solid days with little sleep. They're running through small back alleys strewn with rubble and dead dogs. Every wall of every building has bullet holes in the plaster, revealing patches of brick underneath. The squad runs in a modified wedge with Charlie up front. Intermittent small-arms fire sounds in the distance and it is the only thing he can hear over his own breathing. The heat makes all his gear twenty pounds heavier, and when the sweat saturates his clothes it adds even more weight.

Charlie lifts his left hand and motions for the squad to stop. Across the wide street is the metal door of their objective, a three-story building with over-watch of the mosque in their area of operations. Each man in the squad takes a knee behind some sort of cover.

Charlie's still panting and on every breath he can taste animal rot. He wipes his forehead and squints at a window on the second floor of their building. Two men pull away from sight so fast Charlie wants to doubt he even saw them, but he can't doubt, not here.

Charlie points two fingers of his left hand to his eyes and then points to the window. Specialist Spencer, low to the ground, runs up to the front. The two men lock eyes for a moment before Charlie nods. Spence's right hand moves with purpose to his grenade pouch and produces one 40mm high explosive round. The rest of the squad melt behind whatever cover they can find. Charlie and Spence kneel behind a bullet-ridden refrigerator.

Spence aims his M203 grenade launcher at the window, glances at Charlie one last time, back at his target. There's the click of the trigger, the thud of the round leaving the tube, an immeasurable silence. They are rocked with the combination of the explosion and shock wave. The concussion runs through muscles, tendons, and bone like an electrical current.

As soon as the bricks stop raining, Charlie and his squad run into the blown building. The only sound is their gear bouncing at every stride, that and a few coughs. Entering the building Charlie sees one obvious corpse and a trail of smeared blood. One of the men survived and crawled across the dirty floor to a dark corner, and there he gasps for breath, quick and shallow. Green dishdasha. Low moan. Tears flow in two steady streams over his red, full cheeks and those not sucked in by his flared nostrils drip from his chin.

★★★

His son will not stop crying over this silly little fish named Rainbow. Very slowly, Charlie turns his hand until the fish slides across the meat of his palm and falls into the toilet with a plop. The boy wails.

Charlie kneels next to him and puts a large callused hand on each of his hot cheeks. He moves the boy's face, forcing their eyes to meet. He means to tell him to grow up. He means to say that's how life is. No one said it was fair. He means to tell him that death has always been a part of the equation and the sooner he learned that the better off he would be in life.

But he doesn't say that. Instead, Charlie's hands shake. His eyes well with tears, blurring his son's face.

When the first tear spills down his cheek, Charlie has to check to see what it is. His breathing grows deeper, but in fits, and his nose flares. His son watches him wipe his eyes and for just a fraction of a second Charlie can see him feel just a bit better because he doesn't have to carry the pain of Rainbow's death alone.

Charlie cries more now. He can't stop crying. He pulls his son in for a hug, and there on the linoleum floor of his small apartment's bathroom, they both sob.

The Day I Died

by Matt Fieser

Ten years ago, on a dark, trash covered, hopeless road, in a shithole country that no one cared about then or now, I died. I didn't die like my brothers did on that nightmare evening, but like them, a piece of me is now gone from this earth. What piece exactly I'm not sure, but I do know that I am not whole anymore.

Sometimes I catch myself envying veterans who lost a limb or have a permanent limp because of injuries sustained in combat. I just have intense emotions of anger and hatred and remorse and guilt all mixed up inside me tearing at one another to be released. I do a pretty good job of keeping it bottled up; I store it in that empty piece of me that I left on the killing fields of Baghdad.

Is it crazy that I wish I had lost my leg so that at least I felt like I gave something for this war? Something to show people that, "Hey, I was there, too! I did my part."

What the hell is wrong with me?

Over the years I feel like I have resolved most of my PTSD and survivor's guilt issues. Other times I feel as if nothing has changed. I am constantly replaying that night over, and over, and over in my mind. I fear that other vets think that I didn't do enough that night. A lot of the time I fear the same thing. Dying would have been a whole lot easier than trying to find a way to make sense of how to live like the rest of America does. My self-criticism never ends. I'm my own Dr. Jekyll and Mr. Hyde.

A few years ago, I decided that I was going to forgive myself and be happy, and I am trying. I still think about the boys daily, but it doesn't hurt as much as it used to. I am not sure if it is time, or if it is the old me trying to resurface, trying to break through the layers of guilt and pain. Either way, I am trying. Most days are good, some days are bad, but I haven't given up on being happy and I never will.

✦✦✦

On the 23rd of March, 2008, in the East Rashid district of Baghdad. My squad was conducting an escort mission for a psy-ops unit in our area of operations. It was a boring mission like the majority of them are, nothing crazy, nothing suspicious, just a simple operation to gain information from local nationals on possible identities of the individuals who had been firing mortars at FOB[10] Falcon in the past couple of weeks. We didn't gain any new intel. Go figure.

So, we began our short journey back to our COP[11] so we could finally get some Easter chow and some rest. I also needed to call home and wish my mom a happy birthday, as well as check in and let her know that I was still alive. We started back to the COP a little after 20:00. Specialist Andy Pool and I were in the back of the PL's[12] Bradley listening to "10 Rounds with Jose Cuervo" by Tracy Byrd. We were talking about how badly we wanted to attempt to go ten rounds with the infamous Jose Cuervo when Matt, our interpreter, started to freak out about two men running across the street behind our convoy.

I grabbed the hand mic in the troop compartment and radioed it up to Lieutenant Mason to make him aware of the activity. At the same time I was sending the transmission, our Bradley's machine gun opened fire. Pool and I immediately perked up and tried to scan outside to see through the tiny periscopes so we could assist with the engagement. As we were trying to figure out what the hell was going on, LT Mason came across the headset and told me that he was going to drop ramp and dismount us to the left. I looked at Pool and told him we are going to dismount left and clear whatever we had just shot up. I assumed since our machine gun engaged something that we were going to clear a car or some type of structure.

---

[10] Forward Operating Base
[11] Combat Outpost
[12] Platoon Leader

As the back ramp dropped, Matt, Pool, and I came sprinting out the back to the left side ready to clear when a man, completely naked and engulfed in flames came running back to us.

The man was screaming, "Pool, Feez, HELP ME!! HELP ME!!"

I remember thinking immediately; *did we just shoot up a car with the one dude in Iraq that spoke perfect English?* It still hadn't clicked who that man was. Pool and I started to yell, "Stop drop and roll, stop drop and roll!" We couldn't use a fire extinguisher because we feared that the immediate shock would possibly kill the individual.

As Pool and I watched in horror, this poor man burning alive. First Sergeant Hussein of our Iraqi Police counterparts jumped on top of the man and began to snuff out the flames. That man was the real hero of the evening, he is the man responsible for keeping the burning man alive. I remember moving to the left side of the Bradley and taking a knee to try to figure out exactly what was going on when Pool said, "That's Sergeant McCoy."

I said, "What?"

He repeated again, "That's Sergeant McCoy, look at the tattoo on his arm."

Then I saw it. I saw the feather and three bands tattooed on the man's forearm and I realized who it was. I immediately turned to look the same way our Bradley was facing and 100 meters in front of us, in the middle of the road, shooting flames twenty-five feet into the dry dark sky, was our lead Bradley. The Bradley I was riding in was the trail vehicle in a convoy of five, with about 25-50 meters separating the vehicles, and even though we were only about 200 meters from the lead Bradley, Pool and I didn't hear the EFP[13] explode and rip through the side of it.

---

[13] Explosive Formed Projectile

I remember clicking the "talk" switch on my radio to try to inform the PL what we had on the ground and nothing. I tried again with the same results. While this was happening I began to hear Pool shooting. He was at the front of the Bradley shooting over the nose across the street into a building.

I shouted, "What the fuck are you shooting at!!"

He looked at me and yelled back, "They're shooting at us!"

Then I saw it, tracer rounds flying right over our heads and the familiar sound of an AK-47 spraying away. It was easy to spot the muzzle flashes with the dark Iraqi night sky as the backdrop, so I moved to the front of the Bradley with Pool and began to engage the top windows of the three-story building that was firing on us. As the engagement began about fifteen of the twenty IP's[14] we had with us on the mission ran off and scattered into the darkness of night.

Our mission had changed from clearing a destroyed target to casualty evacuating our dudes.

Farther off to the right side of our Bradley, about twenty-five meters away, were three buildings which appeared to be abandoned houses. I told Pool that we needed to get into one of those houses to get McCoy off the street and establish a CCP[15] for the rest of the men so when our QRF[16] arrived we could load them up and roll to the CSH[17] . Pool and I continued to return fire on the building as we gathered the three or four Iraqi police who didn't flee the scene and moved to the first building. I told Matt to tell the IP's[18] that they were going to clear the house. They looked back eagerly and wide-eyed, I

---

[14] Iraqi Police

[15] Casualty Collection Point

[16] Quick Reaction Force

[17] Combat Support Hospital (pronounce "cash")

[18] Iraqi Police

assume mostly wide-eyed due to fright and the intense situation we had stumbled into.

They started to argue in Arabic, asking for our night vision glasses, since they had none, and I screamed back absolutely not and to get their asses into the house and start clearing. They didn't want to go in the house now, I told them to breach the door and kill anyone inside. Still they were hesitant. The volume of fire increased and from my viewpoint I could see McCoy was still laying in the middle of the street behind our Bradley completely exposed.

I looked to Pool and told him, "Do whatever the fuck you have to, but get these guys into this house and clear it." He nodded and I sprinted back to the Bradley.

Right as I was returning to the Bradley, the back ramp dropped and the LT came out. I told him my radio was down, that McCoy was burned badly, we were trying to get into the building to establish a CCP, and that we were taking fire from 10 o'clock high and that he needs to hose the whole building with the 25-millimeter cannon on the Bradley.

He said, "Roger," and back he went inside.

I hollered over to Mac that he was going to be okay and to hang in there. I started to move back up the right side of our Bradley to continue to engage the targets across the street when I heard a BOOM!!

My heart sank. I thought that an RPG had hit the Bradley. I couldn't help but think, *"Well what the fuck else could go wrong?"*

The LT popped his head out the hatch and hollered down, "Main gun is down." Okay, well, that's not so bad, we still have the coax[19], then silence. The LT popped his head back out and shouted, "Coax is down." Great. Back to just Pool and me and our M4s.

---

[19] A 240C, belt fed, 7.62mm machine gun

About this time Pool came sprinting back to me, "We can't get in."

"Why not!?" I replied.

"All the doors are all chained up, I couldn't shoot them off, either," he responded.

So I decided, fuck it, we are here and we are shooting it out until QRF gets on station. This part gets a little hazy, but I remember multiple times going out into the wide open trying to get the LT's attention and Pool pulling me back behind cover screaming at me that they were still shooting. I remember at one point we talked about just clearing the building, we were taking fire from ourselves, except there was a culvert that separated the two roads that was filled with water, and no way of us crossing without getting shot or drowning in sewage.

So, the gunfight continued. I was at the tail of the Bradley engaging and Pool was at the front. From time to time I would yell over to McCoy to hang in there and then drop a person who was trying to escape out the back side of the building. At one point, I remember looking at Pool firing and all I could think was, A. My wife is going to be pissed that I am going to die here, and B. I really hope I die before Pool does. I didn't want to watch him die.

So I continued to engage targets, and in the middle of firing, I accepted the fact that I was going to die here. Here on this shitty piece of asphalt, in the middle of this God-forsaken country, on a mission that no one back home even cared about. But, when I accepted my sentence of death, I decided that I was going to kill as many of them as I could before they took me.

At about ten minutes into the gunfight, the Bradley suddenly lurched forward and stopped. Since I had no radio communication I didn't know what was going on. Then the Bradley just took off down the street, driving towards our downed vehicle. Pool and I quickly repositioned behind an IP Chevy 2500 and continued to return fire. We were trying to figure out what the hell our Brad was doing. We found out later that the crew saw the rear taillights of the burning vehicle flickering and thought maybe someone inside was still alive, so they were moving up to dismount and see if they could save anyone.

They couldn't.

As Pool and I were still trying to figure out what our Brad was doing, we were also concerned for McCoy who was still in the middle of the road. We didn't have a litter; it was on the vehicle that was on fire.

Out of nowhere a U.S. Soldier came running in our direction. Honestly, with the lead Brad burning so big and bright, he looked like an Angel coming straight out of Hell to help us. It was a tanker from our Charlie Company who happened to be out on patrol near us, heard our calls on the radio and came to assist. The tanker brought with him a litter and a big aid bag, as well as two M1 Abrams battle tanks. I had never been so happy to see a tank in my life. For the first time since the battle broke out, I felt like we were going to make it.

Suddenly, the firing from across the street ceased. As one of the two tanks rolled down the road on the other side of the culvert, the other pulled security by the blast site along with the rest of our platoon that arrived as the QRF. Pool, the Tanker, Matt, and I ran to McCoy to load him up on the litter to move him to some cover and begin to try and treat whatever wounds we could. As we were loading him on the stretcher, our Brad returned to us and dropped ramp so we could load McCoy and take him to the CSH.

I grabbed the head of the litter to the right side; Matt took the head on the opposite side of me with Pool falling in to my rear on the feet – the tanker across from him. As we were loading Mac into the Brad, we discovered the litter was too long to fit straight into the troop compartment, so we had to angle him diagonally with the head of the litter sitting across Matt's lap, and the rest of him across mine and Pools laps. I remember getting in that Brad and just wanting the ramp to close so they couldn't shoot me.

Then I felt like a piece of shit for having that thought, when I had one of my buddies, a dude who was *my* soldier on our first deployment, laying naked and burned across my lap.

As we began to roll to the CSH, I looked at Mac and thought, *"What the fuck? What the fuck just happened? Where are the rest of the guys? They're probably all dead."*

NO DON'T THINK LIKE THAT!! I would tell myself, even though deep down I already knew their fates.

A few times on the way to the CSH, we would take a hard turn and Mac would kind of roll onto me and I would have to roll him back onto the stretcher, and every time I did he would leave chunks of burned flesh on my kit. At one point, he started to cough up red foam. Pool and I thought we had lost him right there in the back of our truck. But suddenly our vehicle slammed to a halt and Pool's rifle fell down onto Macs shins and he was right back with us.

When we arrived at the CSH, there was a medical team waiting with a gurney. We transferred Mac from the vehicle to the gurney and off he went into Baghdad ER. I asked where the rest of the guys were and one of the Docs said they were only alerted to one coming in.

I knew what that meant, but I didn't want to believe. I held out hope that the other guys were okay, had made it out and were with the rest of the platoon. My worst fears were confirmed when one of our squad leaders found us and confirmed that the four other men — SSG Chris Hake, SPC Jose Rubio-Hernandez, PFC Andrew Habsieger, and PV2 George Delgado — were killed in the blast.

From that point forward, it really was a blur. The rest of our company arrived at the CSH along with our Battalion Commander and

Battalion Command Sergeant Major. There were a lot of hugs and a lot of 'what the fuck went down's,' but the thing I remember the most was the silence.

As we waited outside the CSH to see what was going to happen to SGT McCoy, everyone just kind of sat and smoked or dipped and thought about his wife and kids, and the wives and kids of our brothers who were killed. Every time someone new would show up, like our old PL, everyone would get up and hug again.

But still, it was mostly silent.

After a few hours, we were told that SGT McCoy was going to be flown to Germany. So, my platoon and company, along with the other elements from the battalion who came, lined up on both sides of the street that lead to the landing pad for the Blackhawk that was waiting to take Mac to BIAP[20]. We waited patiently for what seemed like forever until a medical crew wheeled Mac out.

We couldn't see him on gurney; he was covered in what looked like a giant black trash bag, with a tube stuck out for him to breathe. As he made his way down the street, every single soldier snapped to the position of attention and rendered a hand salute. It was silent except for the rotors on the helicopter furiously ripping through the now early morning darkness.

Sergeant Steve McCoy made it to Germany, and then back to a burn unit at Brooke Army Medical Center on Ft. Sam Houston in San Antonio, Texas. He sustained burns on roughly ninety percent of his body. Unfortunately, on 10 June 2008, with his wife by his side, Steve passed away due to an infection.

When I heard, that little bit of hope I still had in me died with him. I was hollow inside. I didn't feel anything except for rage and hate and sadness and guilt. And I still do to this day.

---

[20] Baghdad International Airport

In Memoriam

SSG Chris Hake

SPC Jose Rubio-Hernandez

PFC Andrew Habsieger

PV2 George Delgado

SGT Steve McCoy

SGT Dylan Brenner

SPC Scott Farnsworth

BIOS

Antonia Benson - An aspiring poet and songwriter who was raised in the woodsy cityscape of the Portland, Oregon. She has been using writing as a creative outlet and vehicle for self-growth for the past four years.

Brian Turner earned an MFA from the University of Oregon before serving for seven years in the US Army. He was an infantry team leader for a year in Iraq with the 3rd Stryker Brigade Combat Team, 2nd Infantry Division. Prior to that, he deployed to Bosnia-Herzegovina with the 10th Mountain Division (1999-2000). His poetry has been published in *Poetry Daily, The Georgia Review, American War Poems: An Anthology*, and in the *Voices in Wartime Anthology* published in conjunction with the feature-length documentary film of the same name.

Damon Hugh Faust - I served 2000-2006. My first duty station was in Germany with BIG RED One as a 14 R, which is short-range air defense. I basically was a Bradley driver and gunner while I was with 4'3 ADA. I got out in 2003 with the condition of a Try One with the National Guard. In 2003 the wars in Afghanistan and Iraq were in full swing, it was quite difficult to get out of the service at the time, but I found a loophole in the Try One program, which meant I would continue to serve with a guard infantry unit out of California. This sounded pretty good to me, as I heard the Guard was all BBQs and good times. I was mistaken. It was a rapid-deployment air assault unit that in actuality trained as hard, if not harder than, most active duty units. I ended up getting out after my Try One was over. However, six months later I found out my unit would be going to Iraq in support of operation Iraqi Freedom 3. I was soaking in the Sacramento sun that was beaming through the windows and playing Call of Duty when the phone rang. I picked up to my former PLT Sargent-turned-recruiter asking if I was ready to go to Iraq. I responded with a resounding yes, as I felt obligated to this unit. I taught a few of the men how to drive stick, shared first beers with a few, and felt my skills as a soldier would be an asset.

With that, I re-signed for another two years and found myself in Iraq for all of 2005. I was a team leader who achieved the rank of Corporal, only to lose it after myself and my fire team enjoyed some beers after our first firefight.

I exited the US Army in 2006 respectfully, even though I was on the books until 2008.

While in-country I decided I would attend college with the hope of joining the Peace Corp, to use the skills I learned behind the M4 to illicit change through non-violent action.

I spent the next five years upon returning home studying philosophy and cultural anthropology at Oregon State University, not to find employment after school, but for my own edification. I wanted to understand the benevolence I saw in the chaos of war. I ended up with more questions.

While finishing at OSU I began a family with an old high school friend. That marriage failed, as I was still struggling with my issues around PTSD and TBI. Once our first child was born, the focus of our relationship shifted. Prior to becoming parents, the focus of our little family had been on our union and helping me deal with my issues. The world and our family ethos changed with our firstborn. My struggles were no longer at the forefront, it was now our baby girl. I, however, did not catch on to that as quickly as my ex did.

I spend my time now as a volunteer firefighter with a rural fire department and am attempting to create a small non-profit that engages veterans in international medical tours, training remote communities in first aid.

Jacob Meeks - D Co 1/504 PIR, 82nd Airborne 2000-2004

Jacob Meeks is an aid worker, a veteran, an operations professional, a storyteller, a writer and a leader. He has been working for the past seven years as a humanitarian aid worker in a variety of different locations around the world from South Sudan to Lebanon. In the past, he was an infantryman and a veteran of the 82nd Airborne in the US Army, with deployments to Kosovo and Afghanistan. He was also the founder of a Student Veterans group at Portland State University where he received both his Bachelor's and Master's Degrees.

Jake brings a wide variety of experiences with him and as he transitions back to life in the US, he would like to utilize the experiences through storytelling and community engagement.

Jana Mowreader is retired and lives on a small farm south of Portland. She enjoys her dogs, gardening, reading, writing, travel, scuba diving and running her tractor.

Jessica Standifird is a writer, editor, and musician living in Portland, OR. Her work has appeared in *Microfiction Monday Magazine*, *Perceptions: A Magazine for the Arts*, and is upcoming in the *Ladybox Books Zine Trilogy*, and *Unchaste Anthology, V2*. She performs with the dark-cabaret band Bright & Shiny. You can find her at: JessicaStandifird.com and BrightAndShinyMusic.com

Joe Cantrell - I grew up in Cherokee County, Oklahoma. The assumption was that everybody was part Indian, at least the ones whose parents weren't rich, and if there came an opportunity to serve in the military, the only question was, what branch? Meantime, I finished college and was school photographer for six years there in the hometown.

All the men in the family had served in the World Wars except the uncle who'd been the star quarterback and married the aunt who'd been drum major of the college band. Uniforms and service, check that box.

My choice was to be a Naval Aviator, but Florida swamp hay fever distorted my eyeballs. That created astigmatism dangerous to radio towers and Navy trainers. I could have had a soft job somewhere, but asked for a destroyer assigned to Vietnam. First night in coastal waters, the captain ordered us to sail lights-out, 39 mph through fishing grounds full of Vietnamese junks, tiny boats with families aboard eking their living from the ocean. They lived aboard, had no lights at night, were almost invisible to radar in rough seas— and we hit one. I saw the grandma and two small children fly off into the black water. We maintained 39 mph.

The captain came to the bridge and dismissed the incident with, "That's alright, just next time back down and suck them through the propellers. We don't want any survivors filing for damages." What a sense of humor he had. I thought this was a very strange way to help the South Vietnamese save their country for "democracy."

That was how that tour of duty went. Still hoping for a way to worthy contribution in the war, I volunteered for Deep Sea Diving and Salvage Officer School. Had another cush assignment waiting after graduation, but I had to understand Vietnam better. I went to the Pentagon and got my orders changed to the top Navy Diving Unit operating in Vietnam. That time, I went straight into the 1970 Cambodia Invasion, then took over as Skipper of a diving and salvage boat with 35 men under my command, operating independently in the Mekong Delta. What an absurd predicament for all of us, risking 36 lives, and incidentally the boat, to do odd jobs not worth risking one life, much less 35 (in my opinion).

Also, back home my wife disappeared shortly after some guy I never heard of totaled my cherished MG sports car, and I was charged with the accident on my own driving record. The Red Cross somehow traced her from Oklahoma, to Omaha, to Denver, to Los Angeles, to Berkeley, where they knocked on another guy's apartment door. She came to the door in a shortie nightgown, they said, and after they spoke to her, wrote me a "Dear Pig" letter, saying, "Our marriage is irrelevant to my life." Never saw her after that. We divorced by mail, and a year later I got a stack of letters from collection agencies and sheriffs, bringing back her memory. I'd sent all the money I didn't need home for her to live on and save, but she'd spent all of it, maxed out our credit cards, and hadn't paid a cent on them. I was looking at subpoenas for the thousands "I" hadn't paid; the fact that I had no idea those debts existed was immaterial. Oh well. I had just separated from active duty, had some money in the bank, and paid it all off immediately, but my credit was ruined for the next seven years anyhow. That's how it went.

I stayed in Asia with my cameras, living like a peasant, not a typical expatriate. Eventually, I was shooting for Black Star Photo Agency, the top newspapers and magazines in the world, and many other entities, astonishing to a kid from a little town in the Oklahoma Ozarks. I stayed in Asia almost continuously from 1970 to mid-1986, covered many incredible events, saw a lot. After four years sleeping on a straw mat on a bare floor in Manila shanties, I did get an electric fan. That was nice.

I moved from Manila to Portland. What a change. Went to work for Associated Press Portland as a stringer, a person expected to put in regular hours hanging around the office in hope, perhaps, of getting a paid assignment. But the two salaried guys running the office compensated by acting like Olympic Quality Jerks, such immature, dishonest, bigoted creeps, that didn't last long. They loved to joke about Vietnam vets; the real AP Staff guy had apparently justified his despicable behavior for years by claiming that he was a Vietnam Vet Army hero, until I pinned him down demanding where he'd been and what he'd done. Turned out, he hadn't.

I mention this in some detail, because I believe that a large part of the reasons Vietnam vets had so many problems returning to life in the USA, lies in the way we have been treated by the establishment here. The silliness about Jane Fonda and "being spit on in the airport" are, I believe, typical red herrings to divert blame from the people who were happy to send us to the war, but unwilling to inconvenience themselves for us if and when we came home. So much of this cannot be expressed adequately in words, at least not by me. Ergo, I have strived to develop visual language through photography which can say what I need to say in eye-mind intellect. These images are a few letters from that place.

Jonathan Oak is the author of two poetry books, *Sutlee fukt 1* and *Things I Forgot to Say,* as well as the upcoming novel, *Jerry.* He's been living and performing in the Portland area for the last five years. He spent several years working with the VAMP reading series in San Diego and before that was a fixture in the Phoenix poetry and music scene. He was on the 2001 Phoenix Nationals team, the 2002 Mesa Nationals team and acted as performance coach for the Mesa Team in 2003. He hosted a poetry radio show, worked underground theater in San Francisco, ran writing workshops and reading series for over fifteen years and now heads the dark cabaret band Bright & Shiny here in Portland.

Josh Lubin is a writer and events organizer living in Portland, Oregon. He was the host and curator of the weekly performance series Salon Skid Row. His work can be found online and in print in such places as *NAILED Magazine, Criminal Class Anthology #6,* and in several chapbooks. He is currently completing several manuscripts of poetry and prose for publication.

Julie Elefante was born in Port Hueneme, CA, where her parents settled after her dad retired from the U.S. Navy. Her dad was a Navy Seabee, and her mother dutifully followed him around the world with an ever-growing contingent of children. Julie now lives and works as an editor in Phoenix, AZ. She has been a writer since she was six years old when her dad read her first poem and told her she was a good poet--it was all the validation she has ever needed to keep putting words down on paper.

Karla Lee Erdman, BA, MSed, writes in different genres, but enjoys fiction, especially suspense thriller. She teaches high school English and journalism in Bethlehem, Pennsylvania where she resides with her husband, children, and therapy dog. Karla runs a successful book club, *Thursday Night Book Club*, in which she also writes a monthly blog critique. She is currently studying at Wilkes University in the prestigious Maslow Family Graduate Program in Creative Writing.

Kat Altair - I am a Veteran of the Marine Corps. Since getting out I have completed my MA in Counseling and work with a local community non-profit. Although my partner and I and our dog are "transplants" to the area, the Pacific Northwest is, and will always be, home for us.

Matt Fieser is a native Pacific North Westerner who spent 10 ½ years in the United States Army as an Infantryman. In 2016, he earned his Bachelor's Degree from the University of Washington in Media Communications. He is a diehard baseball fan and spends his free time attending games and concerts.

M. F. McAuliffe is co-author of the poetry collection *Fighting Monsters* (Melbourne, 1998) and the artist's book *Golems Waiting Redux* (Portland, 2011), which documented the destruction of an installation of sculpture in downtown Portland.

In 2002 she co-founded Portland-based, multi-lingual *Gobshite Quarterly* with R. V. Branham; in 2008 they co-founded Reprobate / GobQ Books. Her most recent books are *Seattle: A Novella*, and *The Crucifixes and Other Friday Poems*.

Robert Owen is a Vietnam Era veteran and currently leads the non-profit group Soldier Songs and Voices, in Portland, Oregon.

Ryan Holleran is a former infantry-man who found writing a month after returning from Iraq in 2011. He's a queer poet, student, and peace activist living in Portland, OR, who brings writing workshops to Veterans and their families with hopes to expand healing, understanding and war consciousness.

Sally K Lehman is the author of *Small Minutes, The Unit—Room 154, Living in the Second Tense,* and *In the Fat.* She has also been part of the editing team for the anthologies *Bear the Pall, War Stories 2016,* and *War Stories 2017.* She has had poetry and short stories published in several literary magazines including *Perceptions: a Magazine of the Arts, Lunch Ticket, The Coachella Review,* and *The Gravity of the Thing.* She can be found on the web at SallyKLehman.com and InTheFat.com

Sean Davis is the author of The Wax Bullet War, a Purple Heart Iraq War veteran, and the winner of the Legionnaire of the Year Award from the American Legion in 2015, and the recipient of the Emily Gottfried Emerging Leader, Human Rights award for 2016. His stories, essays, and articles have appeared in the Ted Talk book *The Misfit's Manifesto* by Lidia Yuknavitch, Forest Avenue Press anthology *City of Weird, Sixty Minutes*, Story Corps, *Flaunt Magazine, Human* the movie, and much more.

Sigrid Casey is the relative of men who served in WWI, WWII, and Vietnam.

Thomas J. Keating Biography October 2017

Tom Keating, a graduate of Stonehill College, served in the United States Army, in the Republic of Vietnam, from 1969 to 1970. He served with the 47th Military History Detachment, attached with Headquarters and Headquarters Company, 1st Logistical Command, and Headquarters Company, US Army Vietnam, (USARV) also in Long Binh. Twice awarded the Army Commendation Medal for his service in-country.

Honorably discharged, Tom attended Boston University and completed his Master's degree in Education, (Ed.M.) and taught high school in Burlington, MA for eight years.

He made a successful transition from teaching to corporate communications and learning with companies like Wang Laboratories, Digital Equipment Corporation, IBM and EMC corporation. He wrote and produced training and customer videos, internet learning courses and live television broadcasts. He is retired and currently writing a memoir of his military experiences in the US Army from 1968 to 1970.

Tom attended the AGAPE writing program for veterans at Boston College under the direction of Roxana von Kraus in 2016 and was accepted and attended the Joiner Institute Master Writers Class this past June at UMASS, Boston. He and his wife live in Needham, MA. Tom is an active member of the Veterans of Foreign Wars, Post 2498, Needham and works today as a volunteer assisting veterans of all ages.

William Nichols is 42 years old. He has been married to his wonderful wife Heather for 17 years. They have four beautiful children. He is a medically retired Army Veteran with one deployment to Iraq as a Medic in the 82nd Airborne Division. He has exactly ten years of service in the United States Army and is currently a student at Portland State University, working towards a Bachelor's in Fine Arts in Creative Writing.

Our thanks to the following groups for their time and assistance in putting this anthology together

F&J Ravin American Legion Post #134

Oregon
Humanities

WARRIORWriters

PROFILE THEATRE

TKMco
The Kelly Mercantile Company

Made in the USA
Middletown, DE
30 July 2018